Benjamin Franklin De Costa

Sailing Directions of Henry Hudson

Benjamin Franklin De Costa

Sailing Directions of Henry Hudson

ISBN/EAN: 9783337329617

Printed in Europe, USA, Canada, Australia, Japan

Cover: Foto ©Andreas Hilbeck / pixelio.de

More available books at **www.hansebooks.com**

SAILING DIRECTIONS

OF

HENRY HUDSON,

PREPARED

FOR HIS USE IN 1608,

FROM THE

Old Danish of Ivar Bardsen.

WITH

AN INTRODUCTION AND NOTES;

ALSO

A DISSERTATION ON THE DISCOVERY OF THE HUDSON RIVER.

BY THE

REV. B. F. DeCOSTA,

AUTHOR OF THE PRE-COLUMBIAN DISCOVERY OF AMERICA BY
THE NORTHMEN, ETC.

ALBANY:
JOEL MUNSELL.
1869.

PREFACE.

It was the author's intention at the outset to print the treatise of Ivar Bardsen with a few explanatory notes; yet the interest proved such as to induce the author to enlarge the plan and include a dissertation on early voyages to America, with especial reference to the discovery of the Hudson river, together with a new translation from the text as given in *Grönland's Historiske Mindesmærker* and *Rafn's Antiquitates Americanæ*.

The influence of this work on modern cartography would, of itself, afford a fair subject for an essay. But few of those, who in times past used its material at second and third hand, knew anything of the origin of the influence that shaped their views. It is to be regretted, however, that in the day of Torfæus the means of interpreting Bardsen aright had been lost, and that the location of Old Greenland was so long misunderstood. As it was, however, Torfæus knew less of the location of Old Greenland in 1617 than Antonio Zeni in the year 1400. This suggests the high probability that the Zeni brothers became acquainted with Bardsen's treatise, when in Frisland, the *Faroesland or Faröe, whence the original of Henry Hudson's own version came about the year* 1490. At all events, Antonio Zeni had the equivalent of Bardsen's treatise, and drew up his map of Old Greenland by its light, while more modern writers, like Torfæus, were unable to comprehend its purport. Antonio Zeni knew indusputably where Old Greenland lay, which Torfæus *did not;* a fact that is alone sufficient to vindicate the ancient date of his map, — the first, of which we have any knowledge, that shows any part of the continent of America.

STUYVESANT PARK,

NEW YORK, 1869.

CONTENTS.

SAILING DIRECTIONS

OF

HENRY HUDSON.

————•——

INTRODUCTION.

Greenland was first colonized by Eric the Red, a man banished from Iceland for the crime of murder.[1] He sailed from Iceland with a company of his friends in the year 982, saying that he would seek the land formerly seen at the west by Gunnbiorn,[2] when, in the year 876, he was driven away from the Iceland coast in a storm. In due time he reached the eastern shore of Greenland, sailed southward, doubling Cape Farewell, and passed the winter in Ericseya, one of the fiords on the western shore. The following summer he fixed his abode in a place which he called Ericsfiord. It is said

——— —

[1] Christophessen supposed that Greenland was discovered in the year 770, and Pontanus (pp. 97-8) gives the Bull of Gregory IV, in which Greenland is mentioned. The first impression is that the document must be a fraud, but possibly the disagreement may be otherwise explained.

[2] See the notes to the text of Ivar Bardsen's treatise.

that " the same summer he explored the western desert, and gave names to many places."[1] The next winter he spent on an island called Rafns-gnipa, returning the third year to Iceland.

In the summer of the year 986, he sailed for Greenland again with a fleet of thirty-five ships, only fourteen of which reached their destination.

Gradually the colonists multiplied, Christianity was adopted, churches were built, a line of bishops was established, voyages to America were inaugurated, and society took a somewhat settled form.

Eventually, however, the colonies, after surviving for a period of no less than three hundred years, fell into decline, and then became extinct.

The Greenland settlements were divided into two districts, or *bygds*, called respectively the East and the West Bygds. When attention was first called to the subject, it was generally, if not unanimously, believed that the eastern community was located on the east coast of Greenland, and the western on the opposite side of that country. But soon the whole question came into dispute, and the most eminent of the northern scholars and antiquarians united in the discussion. In the end, the old view was found to be untenable.

---

[1] See *Prof. Rafn's Antiquities of America*, p. 12, and the author's work on *The Pre-Columbian Discovery of America by the Northmen*, p. 17.

In order to settle the question still more effectu-
ally, an expedition was dispatched by the king of
Denmark in the year 1828, with instructions to
proceed to Greenland and explore the entire eastern coast, thus ascertaining by a practical survey
whether it was once inhabited or not. The person
placed in command of this expedition was Captain
Graah, an officer well fitted for the work by his
courage, prudence and capacity. His explorations
extended through a period of two years, in which
time he performed all that, under the circumstances, any individual could have accomplished.

Starting from Friedericksthal with two boats,
manned chiefly by natives, he passed around Cape
Farewell, and made his way, with much labor and
peril, along the eastern coast, exploring the bays
and fiords in search of some memorial of the Northmen, who were said to have formerly lived there.
Spending two summers, and extending his search
as far northward as latitude 65° 30', he was
finally obliged to return to Friederichsthal, without discovering a single indication pointing to the
former occupation of that part of the country by
Europeans.

This region indeed proved less inhospitable than
was generally supposed, and notwithstanding the
too unapproachable character of the coast, it was
found to be not altogether destitute of inhabitants.

Here and there he discovered a handful of natives, who subsisted on the products of the land and sea; yet it was clear from what he saw that no considerable European population could possibly have remained there long. Besides, the natives themselves, who were perfectly acquainted with every foot of the territory, had never seen or heard of ancient ruins of any kind, and had no tradition of a European settlement.

After the publication of the results of Captain Graah's explorations, nearly all of those who had formerly held the old view gradually gave it up, and to-day it would perhaps be impossible to find a student of northern antiquities who maintains the Icelandic occupation of the eastern coast.[1]

Besides, the accounts which exist in the Icelandic chronicles evidently teach that both the East and West Bygds were located on the opposite side of Greenland, and nothing but a misapprehension of the text of the manuscripts led scholars for a time to think otherwise.

The fullest account of the colonies in Greenland is given by Ivar Bardsen or Boty, who, while gene-

---

[1] The learned Asher of Amsterdam indeed supposes that the settlements were on the east coast, but he does not appear to have attended much to the history of Greenland. His erroneous view obscures his discussion on p. cxliii of his *Henry Hudson*.

rally correct in his statements, nevertheless falls into some errors. This, however, is not of much consequence, for the reason that still earlier writers afford the means of making the necessary corrections. In the notes which accompany the text of Bardsen his errors will be pointed out. Considering the character of the times in which he wrote, his account must be accepted as exceedingly intelligent and fair.

Of the narrative or treatise of Ivar Bardsen we have several versions. One is given in the learned Prof. Rafn's great work, *Antiquitates Americanæ*,[1] and a translation in *Purchas His Pilgrimes*.[2] It is there stated that it was translated out of the Norsh[3] language into high Dutch in the year 1560, and from the high Dutch into the low Dutch by William Barentson, which copy was preserved by Jodocus Hondius to be translated into English by William Stere in 1608, for the use of Henry Hudson.

The interest of this document consists, first, in its antiquity, since it far ante-dates the age of Colum-

[1] P. 300.—See version, in *Grönland's Hist. Mindesmærker*.

[2] Vol. III, pp. 518–21.

[3] Prof. Rafn's version is in an antiquated Danish, which is probably meant by *Norsh*. The language of the Northmen is most properly known as the *Old Northern*, or *Dönsk tünga*. It is now spoken in Iceland alone.

bus. The substance of it also exists in the ancient *Landanama-bok*, or Dooms-day book of Iceland. Second, as it comes in the version of Purchas, with all its changes, corruptions and additions, it is a literary curiosity. And in the third place it has a deep interest, with those who admire ancient things, on account of its association with Henry Hudson, who carried it with him on one or more of his voyages. Dr Asher, the accomplished editor of *Henry Hudson the Navigator*, published by the Hakluyt Society, prints the treatise in the appendix to his valuable work, but he does not notice its chief interest. The reason of this is perhaps to be found in the fact that the history of the document has not been thoroughly understood heretofore, except by northern antiquarians like Professors Rafn, and Magnusson, who also have failed to point out at large its connection with the famous Englishman. While interested in the exploits of Bardsen, these scholars were not particularly drawn to Hudson. Yet the select number into whose hands this little work is liable to fall will perhaps take a kindly interest in both, and find some material for thought in the fact that the renowned English navigator, whose name will forever be linked with the history of America, sailed for the northern parts of this continent, carrying with him the sailing directions used in the Pre-

Columbian age by the Northmen in their voyages from Norway and Iceland to the Greenland coast.

Of Henry Hudson little is known. He appears for a brief time, and then vanishes. We know that he was an Englishman who had one or more children, though nothing positively certain can be gleaned in regard to his lineage. After a careful investigation, Mr. Read in his interesting work on Hudson concludes that he may have been the grandson of Henry Hudson an alderman of London who died in 1555, being one of the founders of the Muscovy Company. John, the son of the first mentioned Henry Hudson, was alive in 1618, living in London. It is possible that Henry Hudson the Navigator was born " within the sound of Bow Bells." His whole life, as known to us, extends only through a period of four years. We see him first in the Church of St. Ethelburge, London, with his crew, receiving the sacrament prior to setting out on his first voyage, and we view him for the last time drifting away in an open boat on the cold North sea.

His first voyage was made in 1607 for the Muscovy Company, in search of a north-east route to China along the coast of Spitzbergen. The second, in 1608, was for the same purpose, and led him to the region of Nova Zembla. The third voyage, performed at the expense of the Dutch

East India Company, was made in 1609. He
first sailed north-east, where he was repulsed by
the ice near Nova Zembla, and then sailed west,
reaching our own shores, and exploring the Hudson.   In 1610, Hudson again sailed to search for
a north-west passage, the expense of the voyage
being borne by three English gentlemen, when
he explored the bay and strait that bear his name,
passing the winter of 1610–11 in the southern
part of the bay.   On June 21st, he was set adrift
with his son and seven companions, in an open
boat, never afterward to be seen.

In his third voyage he probably had with him
the sailing directions of Ivar Bardsen, though on
that occasion he did not come in sight of the
Greenland coast.   During the fourth voyage Greenland was seen June 4th, in latitude 65°, where he
was "encumbred with much ice."   When the muti-
neers were returning to England with Hudson's
ship, they saw "the Desolations," or the southern
part of Greenland.   Abacuk Prickett says "this
land is a great iland in the west part of Groneland."   In the notes an explanation of the origin
of this name will be given.   From the Desolations
Hudson had made his way through the strait that
bears his name.

Of what practical use the directions of Bardsen
proved we are not able to say, yet it is reasonable

to infer that they were consulted, from the fact that they were translated for his special benefit. Under the circumstances, he would not have overlooked any suggestions, though he probably did not have the faintest suspicion of their practical value. Besides, it is probable that he viewed the Greenland of Ivar Bardsen as extending around to the region of Spitzbergen and Nova Zembla. At least such was the common view at the time. If he had not understood Bardsen as describing the eastern coast of Greenland, but had caught at his real meaning, his fourth voyage would have had an entirely different termination, and possibly produced much more good. If he had known that colonies existed for the space of three hundred years on the western coast of that southern region of Greenland, then called Desolations, he would have sought the old Icelandic track, and taken the course which they pursued in their high northern explorations, making his way towards Lancaster sound; and when there, enlightened by the experience of three hundred years, he would have abandoned the delusion of a practical north-west passage, returning at last, perhaps, to his home, publishing those discoveries concerning the Northmen that Egede afterwards gave to the world. But this was not to be. A mournful fate awaited him in that dreary clime. In the meanwhile he was to rove in the south.

Starting from Amsterdam March 25, 1609, he sailed first for Nova Zembla in search of an opening to the Flowery Kingdom. Here the unbroken ice barriers opposing his progress, and his men becoming dissatisfied, he gave them their choice of sailing to Davis's straits, to seek a north-west passage, or of going to the American coast in latitude forty. They voted in favor of the latter proposition, and though Hudson's instructions, received from his superiors, enjoined his return to Holland, in case the north-east passage could not be effected, he deliberately disobeyed, and turned the prow of the Half Moon towards the west.

When the heights of Greenland came in view he veered to the south. Reaching the latitude of Mount Desert, on the coast of Maine, he delayed in that romantic region to step a new fore-mast. He next sailed down the coast near the borders of Virginia, and returning, entered Delaware bay. Continuing his northward course, he found the bay of New York, and, September, 1609, dropped anchor inside, off Sandy hook. Delaying here only a few days, he entered the river, passed the Palisades, wound his way through the Highlands and reached the limit of navigable water. It is pleasant to follow, in imagination, and view him as he appears in Talbot's noble picture sailing up this stream. It is the nut-brown month of September, and the birchen

trees are beginning to glow with autumnal splendor,
while the sky, filled with lazily floating clouds, is
already dreaming of the evening hour. The savages flock to the banks, and embark in their canoes,
to follow the ship of the Manitou, which, borne less
by wind than tide, slowly makes her way along
under the noble Palisades, now flinging themselves
down at full length on the calm, pulseless tide.
The quaint little Half Moon, which afterwards, in
1616, disappeared on the coast of Sumatra, no longer
tosses among the bergs of Zembla, but sluggishly
heads up what Hudson may have hoped was the
passage to India. Yet in the end, whatever may
have been his hopes, he was undeceived; and after
thoroughly exploring the river he set sail for home.

Thus, though he failed to find a route to India,
the popular notion is that he first discovered that
noble stream, which, born among the peaks and
passes of the Adirondacks, flows majestically on
through those lovely scenes which it partially
creates, until it loses itself in the sea. And since
some scholars are of the same opinion, let us
briefly inquire into its worth, at the same time al-
luding to various early voyages to America.

We have already stated the probabilities in
regard to the degree of practical influence that
Bardsen's work had upon Hudson. He held the
key to old Greenland in his hand, but he does not

appear to have understood its use. But let us
glance also at the case of others.

It has often been asked if Columbus gained any
information from the Icelanders when, in the year
1477, he visited that country. This does not appear probable, for the reason that if he had obtained any information it would have doubtless
been in substance that given by Ivar Bardsen.
Columbus, of course, knew nothing of the Icelandic, and he could not always be sure of meeting an Icelandic navigator who spoke Latin, or his
own tongue. If he had obtained the old sailing
directions, he would probably, in his age, have followed them. In that case, he would have sailed
between Iceland and the Faröe island until he
sighted Greenland; then, coasting south, doubled
the ancient Hvarf at Cape Farewell, and afterwards sailed into Ericsfiord or some of the higher
bays. As it was, however, he had no conception
of land in that direction, and sailed boldly west
past the Canaries, until he reached the island of
Hispaniola, which, to the day of his death, he
firmly believed constituted the western part of the
East Indies.

In regard to Sebastian Cabot the evidence is
clearer. For aught we know he might have received instructions from the Icelandic sailors who
in his day frequented the port of Bristol, England;

and when he actually went forth, reaching the American continent fourteen months before it was seen by Columbus, he took substantially the course of the old Northmen.

In this connection it is interesting to note the fact that Sir John Barrow, in his *Chronological History of Voyages to the North-west*, adduces a Pre-Columbian voyage by John Vaz Costa Cortereal, a gentleman of the household of the infanta, Don Fernandez. This person, on the return from the voyage, was appointed governor of Terceira, one of the Azores. His commission was dated at Evora, April 12, 1464. The statement rests on the authority of the Portuguese writer, Cordeyro. Biddle, laboring in the interest of Cabot, attacks Sir John Barrow with that partisan warmth which leads us sometimes to suspect the fairness of his statements, and declares (*Life of Cabot*, p. 283), that Sir John had not even looked into Cordeyro's work. Major, however, in the introduction to his *Letters of Columbus* (p. xxxi), doubts Biddle's statement; but, in defending the priority of Columbus's claim, also questions the voyage of Costa Cortereal, who is represented at that time as seeking a north-west passage.

First, it is said, that in his commission as governor of Terceira there is no recognition of his voyage. But at that early time the voyage may not have appeared so particularly meritorious; while, if it had been, it is not so certain that it would gain mention. Again, it is said that his attempt to make a north-west passage, took for granted the existence of a large body of land lying in the region of America.[1] But Major does not prove that the knowledge of that land was totally unknown in Europe. In the eleventh century, Adam of Bremen knew of the existence of that land, which was called Vinland. Major, somewhat in opposition to Biddle, says that that Cordeyro was a respectable historian, and that the whole question turns on his account. The fact that no notice of the voyage is found in the catalogues of Lisbon voyages between 1412 and 1640 is hardly conclusive. Costa Cortereal may have had access to some of the sailing directions of the Northmen, while we actually find Gomera mentioning the navigator John Kolnus, who in the year 1476 was clearly sent to Greenland by the Danish king, Christian I, who reigned in Denmark and Norway. This is declared by various old writers. Wytfliet, in his *Descriptionis Ptole-*

---

[1] By conceding the authenticity of the Zeni chart, which was certainly drawn up from Icelandic authorities, and upon which Hudson, in turn, *largely based his own map*, the difficulty, if it be a difficulty, entirely disappears, since the Estotiland of the Zeni was a part of America.

maicre Augmentum, published in 1603, after speaking of the voyage of the Zeni brothers to Greenland, tells us that the second person to rediscover that country was John Skolnus, the Pole, who, in the year 1476, being in the service of King Christian, sailed beyond Iceland and Greenland, and landed on Labrador, the Estoliland of the Zeni brothers.[1]

Humboldt accepts this voyage as authentic, remarking, " Skolny was in the service of Christian II,[2] of Denmark, in 1476, and they say that he sailed past the coast of Norway, Greenland and Frisland of the Zeni, and landed upon the shore of Labrador." Yet he is in doubt, in regard to Skolnus having reached Labrador, and says: " I cannot hazard any opinion on the statement made to this effect by Wytfliet, Pontanus and Horn. A country seen after Greenland, may, from the direction indi-

[1] The following is the language of Wytfliet : Secundum detectæ huius regionis decus tulit Johannes Scolnus Polonus, qui anno reparate salutis M. CCCC. LXXVI. Octoginta & sex anius á primâ eius lustratione nauigans vltra Nouegiam, Greenlandiam, Frislandiamque, Boreale hoc fretum ingressus sub ipso Arctico circulo, ad Labaratoris hanc terram Estotilandiamque delatus est, multo deinde tempore intentatum hoc nautis mansit littus dum algentis climatis gelu, aut infesti maris horrent procellis haud satis dignum ob præmium (p. 102). Pontanus (p. 765) quotes the account of Wytfliet with approval.

[2] Both Humboldt and Major make the mistake of putting this event in the reign of Christian II. Christian I reigned from 1448 to 1481.

cated, have been Labrador.   I am, however, sur-
prised to find that Gomara [chap. xxxvii] who published his *Historia de las Indias* at Saragossa in 1553,
was cognizant even at that time of this Polish pilot.
It is possible that when the codfishery began to bring
the seamen of southern Europe into more frequent
connection with the Scandinavian sailors, a suspicion may have arisen that the land seen by Skolny
must have been the same as that visited by John
Cabot in 1497, and by Gaspar Cortereal in 1500.
Gomara says, what in other respects is not quite
right, that the English took much pleasure in fre-
quenting the coast of Labrador, for they found the
latitude and the climate the same as that of their
native land, *and that the men of Norway have been
there too with the pilot, John Skolny,* as well as the
English with Sebastian Cabot."   Humboldt adds
to this : " Let us not forget that Gomara makes no
mention of the Polish pilot with reference to the
question of the priority of Columbus, though he is
malignant enough to assert, that it is in fact impossible to say to whom the discovery of the New
Indies is due." (*Examen Critique,* vol. II, p. 153–4.)
    The sentence given from Gomara by Humboldt,
is found in chapter xxxvii of his *General History
of the Indies.*   In chapter xxxix he also remarks
that Bretons and Danes have likewise gone to the

Bacaloas. Kunstmann also calls attention to the subject in his work, *Die Entdeckung Amerikas*.

He says (p 45): On historical grounds, however, is a voyage hitherto too little noticed, which was undertaken by the men of the north who formerly visited the coast of America from Norway in the second half of the fifteenth century." He then continues: " Francis Lopez Von Gomara, so called from the name of one of the Canary islands where he was born, had, according to his own testimony, obtained from Olaus of Gotha much knowledge about the condition of Norway and her shipping. We may thank him for the information given in his *Description of Labrador*, that the men from Norway and the pilot, John Skolnus, and the English with Sebastian Cabot had visited there."

In support of the voyage of Kolnus, we have the map of Michael Lok, of the date of 1527, as given in *Hakluyt's Divers Voyages touching the Discoverie of America*, which was printed in 1582. This map, Lok says, was based by him upon a map drawn at Seville, and presented to Henry VIII. by Verrazano. A large tract of land, which appears to be the same as that now known as Baffin's Land, is marked, "Jac. Scolvum, Groesland."

The voyage of Skolnus does not, however, appear much like a marvel, when we remember that for centuries prior to his time the communication was maintained with more or less regularity. The last of the seventeen bishops of Greenland, Andreas, was sent over in the year 1406, and three years later we have the proof of a marriage performed by him in the Cathedral of Gardar. Moreover Wormius told Peyrere (*Egede's Greenland*, p. xlvii) that down to the year 1484 there was a company of sailors at Bergen in Norway who still traded with Greenland. The Icelander, Biœrn von Skardfa, also speaks of a Hamburg sailor, who sailed in the North seas at about this period, whose adventures had earned for him the name of Jon Greenlander.

It is proper here, however, to notice the fact that Peyrere had scruples about what Wormius told him of the Bergen sailors; yet the only argument that has been brought against it rests on the fact that in Queen Margaret's reign, 1389, some Norway merchants fell under the ban of the law for sailing to Greenland without the royal license. This fact, almost accidentally preserved, helps, instead of conflicting with, the statement of Wormius that trade was carried on in 1484. Yet it is a fact that communication had ceased about the year 1500. Nevertheless, the truth that a great continent lay in the ocean at the west, was still familiar to a class of Scandinavian

minds; for when in the year 1513, King Christian II ascended his throne, he bound himself
with a solemn vow to reopen the ancient communication with Greenland. At the same
time, Eric Walkendorf entered upon the work
with much enthusiasm, but, eventually sharing
the misfortunes of his sovereign, he went to
Rome, where he died without accomplishing his
purpose.

When, therefore, we consider the whole question,
the alleged voyage of Costa Cortereal, in 1464,
does not appear at all improbable;[1] since he may
have conferred with some one of the Scandinavian
sailors then voyaging to Greenland, and, on the information thus gained, embarked in an expedition
of his own, which at that time might easily have
passed as an event of minor importance to the
world, and thus gained no prominent place in the

_____

[1] In this connection it may be of interest to note the fact
that the author of a privately printed work on Columbus (p. 82)
speaks as follows: "Santarem quotes two works: One by Eras-
mus Shmid (*apud* Fabricius *Bib. grœc.*, I, 145), which tends
to show that Homer was aware of the existence of this continent; the other, by De Guignes, *Remarques Geographiques et
Critiques*, from which we learn that the Chinese had established
important commercial relations with America as early as the
year 458 of our era." Which of Santarem's works are referred
to, he does not state. There is no doubt much valuable material
is stored up in the Chinese archives, which in course of time will
be brought to light.

chronicles of the day.[1]   It may, therefore, yet be demonstrated to the satisfaction of historical students that the old sailing directions of Bardsen were known by a few on the European continent in those early days of the Cortereals.[2]   And it is of sufficient interest to mention in this connection

---

[1] If Columbus had been familiar with the Icelandic, he might have gained this knowledge for himself, when, *the very year following the voyage of Skolnus* he sailed far into the north and visited Iceland.

In the year 1477 he wrote to his son Ferdinand, that " he sailed a hundred leagues beyond the isle of Thule, the southern part of which is distant from the equinoctial line seventy-three degrees, and not sixty-three as some assert; neither does it lie within the line which includes the west of Ptolemy, but is much more westerly.   To this island, which is as large as England, the English, especially those from Bristol, go with their merchandise.   At the time that I was there the sea was not frozen, but the tides were so great as to rise and fall twenty-six fathoms.   It is true that the Thule, of which Ptolemy makes mention, lies where he says it does, and by the moderns it is called Frislandia ; " that is, *Faroesland*, or Faroe   We may remember here also that the Bristol traders saved Iceland from the fate which overtook Greenland.   For letter of Columbus, see *Select Letters of Columbus*, p. xlv, by Major.

[2] " The family name was originally *Costa* or *Coste*, and is of French extraction, having come to Portugal along with Count Alphonzo Henriquez, under whom one of the Costas served in the taking of Lisbon and conquering Portugal from the Moors. The family settled in Algarve, and when John Vaz Costa (some say his father) came to the Portuguese court, he used to live in such splendor and hospitality that the king observed to him, ' Your presence, Costa, makes it a *real Court*.' "   *Major's Letters of Columbus*. p. xlvii.

the testimony of Las Casas, who saw a work by Columbus[1] himself, *On the Information gathered from Portuguese and Spanish Pilots concerning Western Lands* (See *Notes on Columbus*, privately printed, Astor Library, p. 85). This seems to indicate very clearly that *something* was known by the Spanish and Portuguese; and possibly, when the treatise referred to by Las Casas comes to light from among the rubbish of some old library where it is now buried, we may *find the name of John Vaz Costa Cortereal written therein.*

But we must now turn to Henry Hudson. The character of Hudson, judged by the age in which he lived, was tolerably fair, though, of course, hardly superior to ordinary examples. If it is true, as Mr. Read supposes, that Hudson was nurtured under the influences of the Muscovy Company which Alderman Hudson helped to form, we should prefer to have seen him adhering to the service of the English, instead of taking the pay of the Dutch in his third voyage. But for this change he doubtless had satisfactory reasons. It has also been remarked that in his third voyage he disobeyed his orders. On this point we may conclude that he was quite

---

[1] Columbus first thought of land at the west in 1470. In 1473 he received a map relative to the subject from the Florentine astronomer, Toscanelli.

as capable of judging as the Company.   His insub-
ordination was, on the whole. beneficial.   In his last
and fatal voyage, it is said that he secretly amassed a
large quantity of the ship's stores. after having pro-
fessed to have made an equal distribution of all the
provisions on board.   This was doubtless with the
best of intentions, since, if he did not ultimately
share them with his men, it must have been clear to
his mind that he could never bring his ship into port.
He also fell into needless trouble with the natives,
which cost lives, and allowed some of them to
become intoxicated on board the Half Moon, where
in her little cabin, they held an unseemly revel.
This, however, was a mistake of judgment.   He
lived in an age much ruder than ours, a time when
manners on ship-board were more generally de-
praved.   On the whole, Hudson was hardly a man to
be spoken against.   But, on the other hand, his character does not demand the high praise which some
have given.   He was of fair courage, and persever-
ing, but not original or great, in any sense of the
terms.   His was a respectable mediocrity.   In
navigation he had no new conceptions, but was
rather a copyist.   This being so, we might infer
at the outset, that he was not the first to discover
the river which bears his name.   We find even
that the voyage to this latitude was suggested by
another.

This was his friend, Captain John Smith, who argued that in latitude forty he would find a passage to India. The influence of Weymouth, to whose voyage he had access through Plantius, appears to have been considerable; while he may also have seen the globe made by Euphrosynus Vlpius of Venice, in 1542, which lays down a narrow strait leading westward in the latitude of the Hudson river. Hudson must certainly have been acquainted with the map of Michael Lok, published in Hakluyt's work of 1582, and Wytfliet's of 1603. The map of Norumbega and Virginia, given by the latter, though wrong in the calculation of latitudes, shows that navigators were then perfectly familiar with the coast. On this map Cape Hatteras and Chesapeake bay are laid down under those names, while the map of Lok shows numerous inlets between Florida and New York, among which there is no difficulty in finding Delaware bay. But in conducting the inquiry let us first ascertain what were the early opinions in regard to the priority of the voyage of Hudson.

The common representation teaches that, according to the tradition of the Indians, Hudson was the first European that visited this river, the beautiful Cohotatea of the aborigines. Yet this is simply a partial view, obtained for political use, and is manifestly untrue; for no less a personage

than Petrus Stuyvesant, the governor of New
Amsterdam, himself admitted that the Dutch were
not the first visitors, and inclined to award this
honor to the French. Among other testimonies
we have that of the Dutch Labadists, who came
to New Amsterdam in 1679. Their journal, re-
cently translated from the Dutch by Mr. Murphy,
for the Long Island Historical Society, contains the
very interesting statement, that when they visited
Long Island the Indians told them that the first
strangers "seen in these parts" were " Spaniards
or Portuguese," but that they did not remain long,
and that "*afterwards*" the Dutch came. (*L. I.
Hist. Coll.*, vol. I, p. 273). This alone stamps the
story of Van Der Donk with its true character
where he makes the natives declare that they
"*did not know there were any other people in the
world*" before the Half Moon arrived (*N. Y. Hist.
Coll.*, ser. II, p. 137).

Afterwards the Labadists went to Albany, and
on the west side of the river, just below the town,
they saw the remains of an old fort " built as they
[the people] say, by the Spaniards." (*L. I. Hist.
Coll.*, vol. I, p. 318). Here, then, we have the Spaniards again, though the notion that the fort was
built by them appears to be sufficiently well dis-
posed of by the fact presented by Mr. Brodhead
in his *History of New York* (p. 55), where we find

that Hendrick Christiaensen built a fortified trading house on the island referred to, in 1614. It had a strong stockade, a moat eighteen feet wide, and was armed with two large guns and eleven swivels. Still, though it is clear that the tradition in regard to the Portuguese and Spaniards, existed when the Labadists visited Albany, we must not, at a time like the present, when American history is freeing itself from the meshes of fable, allow ourselves to fall into the error of bringing a tradition to prove a *fact*, but we should rather use facts to prove the *tradition*. Let us therefore inquire what it is really worth.

First, then, we find that the priority of Hudson's discovery is denied by the Dutch themselves, who, according to Dr. O'Callaghan (*New Netherland*, p. 26), had two ships, those of Sieur Beveren, sailing in American waters in 1512. Of course we have no knowledge of the particular places visited. But when we come to the period of 1598 the statements assume a tangible form. In the year 1644, the committee of the Dutch West India Company, known as the General Board of Accounts, to whom numerous documents and papers had been intrusted, made a lengthy report, which they begin by saying: "New Netherlands, situated in America, between English Virginia and New England, extending from the South [Delaware] river, lying

5

in 34½ degrees, to Cape Malabar, in the latitude
of 41½ degrees, was first frequented by the inhabitants of this country in the year 1598. and especially by those of the Greenland Company, but
without making any fixed settlements, only as a
shelter in the winter. For which they erected on
the North (Hudson) and South (Delaware) rivers
there two little forts against the incursions of the
Indians." (*N. Y. Col. Doc.*, vol. 1, 149).[1]

This testimony, which we have no means of dis-
proving, sweeps away at a single blow the claim of
Hudson as the discoverer of the *Cohotatea* of the Indians, as well as that of the noble Delaware; and
so far as the Englishman may be concerned, we
might well rest the case where the committee of the
West India Company leave it in their report to the
states-general. But there are other claims to be
considered.

We must pass over the statements of Holmes,
Chalmers and others, that Cabot, who sailed down
the American coast to the latitude of Gibraltar,
made himself acquainted with all this part of the

<hr/>

[1] On this testimony Mr. Brodhead says, in his *History of New
York* (p. 35 *n.*), that the statement " needs confirmation," and
refers (in Appendix A) to *N. Y. Hist. Soc. Proc.*, app. 96; *N.
Y. Lit. World*, No. 322, p. 271; *N. A. Rev.*, 1x, 163–165;
and Heckewelder, in *N. Y. Hist. Coll., series* II, vol. 1, 71–73.
None of these references, however, conflict with the Dutch report, which, being based on documents, and coming from

continent, for the reason that we do not know what
he actually accomplished, and come to Verrazano,
who is generally believed to have explored the
coast in 1524. If the record is authentic, it must
also be admitted that this navigator, who made himself so famous as Juan Florentin, actually entered
the bay of New York and discovered the mouth of
the river. His alleged letter to Francis I, king of
France, dated July 8, 1524 (see *N. Y. Hist. Coll.*, ser.
II, vol. I, p. 45), states that in sailing northward
along the coast, evidently in the region of New
York, he " found a very pleasant situation among
some steep hills, through which a very large river,
deep at its mouth, forced its way to the sea ; to the
estuary of the river, any ship heavily laden might
pass with the help of the tide, which rises eight feet.
But as we were riding at anchor in a good berth,
we would not venture up in our vessel, without a
knowledge of the mouth ; therefore we took the
boat, and entering the river, we found the country
on its banks well peopled, the inhabitants not dif-
fering much from the others [previously mentioned]

an honorable body, seems entitled to credit. Heckewelder, in
the above reference, simply gives the Indian tradition of the
arrival of Hudson, which, without saying so, appears to teach
that Hudson was the first European who came to the river.
But we have already seen, from the forced admission of the
too partial Van Der Donck, that such was *not* the unanimous
belief among the natives.

being dressed out with the feathers of birds of
various colors. They came forward towards us
with evident delight, raising loud shouts of admiration, and showing us where we could most se-
curely land with our boat. We passed up this
river about half a league, when we found it formed
a most beautiful lake three leagues in circuit, upon
which they were rowing thirty or more of their
small boats, from one shore to the other, filled with
multitudes who came to see us. All of a sudden,"
he says, "as is wont to happen to navigators, a violent
contrary wind blew in from the sea, and forced us
to return to our ship, greatly regretting to leave this
region which seemed so commodious and delightful,
and which we supposed must also contain great
riches, as the hills showed many indications of
minerals." Here the description will be recognized
as tolerably good, while the reference to minerals
agrees with the impression received by Hudson when
he looked upon the white-green cliffs near the
Elysian Fields at Hoboken. (See *Brodhead*, p. 34,
and *Asher's Hudson*, p. 90). Leaving New York,
this voyager professes to have sailed northward to
Rhode Island, and from thence passed on to Maine,
where the coast is well described.

Verrazano was an officer in the privateer service
of Francis I. In 1523 he captured two ships sailing from Mexico to Spain, freighted in part with

the arms and jewels of Montezuma and his lords. The capture enabled him to make princely presents to the king and nobility of France.[1] It has been conjectured that he was hanged for piracy, about the year 1527–8.

But the discovery of the Hudson does not depend even upon Verrazano. We have another early navigator, who sailed upon these coasts, in the person of Estevan Gomez. Sir John Barrow says in his *Chronological Account of North-western Voyages* (p. 54), that Gaspar Ens is the only writer who mentions Gomez at all. And yet Gomez is no myth, as we shall see. Purchas's account, taken from the brief tract of Gaspar Ens, published at Cologne, in 1612, is very meagre, yet the voyage of Gomez is perfectly well known,[2] though not mentioned by various prominent writers. In 1519

---

[1] Those who desire to read what is to be said against the authenticity of the Verrazano letter, are referred to the searching paper of Buckingham Smith, Esq., who is so eminently qualified by his researches in this department to speak on the subject.

[2] The references Biddle gives are the following, which all bear on Gomez: *Peter Martyr*, dec. vi, c. x, and dec. viii, c. x; *Oriedo (General History)*, c. x; *Ramusio*, vol. III, p. 52, in Index, title *Stephano; Gomara*, c. xl; *De Bry (Gr. Voy.)*, pt. iv, p. 69; *Funes (History of the Indies)*, fol. 49; *Herrera*, dec. III, lib. VIII, c. viii; *Galvano (Hakluyt, 1601)*, p. 66; *Eden (Decades)* fol. 213; *Sir William Monson (Naval Tracts)*, b. IV. To these may be added *Wytfleet*, p. 101.

he sailed as the chief pilot of Magellan, but finally left him at the Magellan straits under unfortunate, if not disreputable circumstances, and returned home. After finding him engaged in that southern expedition, it is not difficult to believe that he subsequently explored the northern parts of the American coast.

Galvano says of Gomez that, failing to obtain a command in the new expedition to the Moluccas in 1524, he went to the northern coast of America to search for a new passage to those islands. The "Earle Don Fernando de Andrada, and the Doctor Beltram, and the marchant Christopher de Sarro, furnished a gallion for him, and he went from Groine in Galicia to the island of Cuba, and to the point of Florida, sailing by day because he knew not the land. He passed the bay of Angra, and the river Enseada, and so went over to the other side. It is also reported that he came to Cape Razo, in 46 degrees to the north ; from whence he came backe againe to the Groine laden with slaves. In this voyage Gomez was ten monthes."[1]

It was the theory of Gomez, that as when with Magellan he found a southern strait leading to the Indies, so he would now find a short route to the

[1] *Hakluyt's Selections*, ed. 1812, p. 34; *Peter Martyr*, decade VIII, p. 601 ; *Gomara*, lib. I. cap. v.   These are the references of Galvano.

same place by searching the American coast at the
north. He accordingly obtained a caravel. and set
out. according to Navarrete, in February, 1525, to
perform the voyage. He failed to find any opening to the Indies. but nevertheless explored a great
portion of the coast and discovered the Hudson.
Of this the most satisfactory proof exists.[1]

His voyage was of importance for the reason that
it convinced several of the continental governments
of the folly of searching any longer for that unreal
passage which employed the best energies of the
Dutch and English for nearly a century afterwards.
But let us now speak of the expedition more in detail.

Estevan Gomez was a Portuguese sailor in the
service of Spain. In 1524 he attended the congress
at Badajos, Sebastian Cabot likewise being present.
At this congress. Portugal, being jealous of the influence of Spain, opposed the plan for an expedition
to the Indies; but soon after the difficulties between the powers were adjusted. and the king
of Spain, in connection with some merchants, fitted
out a caravel, as already stated. giving Gomez the
command.

Peter Martyr having described the council of
Badajos. held in 1524, which dispatched a fleet to

---

[1] See *Lopez* (*History of India*), ed. 1555, c. 12, 40; *Oviedo*
(*History of India*), 1537, tom. II, lib. XXI, c. 8–9; *Asher's Henry
Hudson*; pp. lxxxvii, cxlv; *Historical Magazine*, 1866, p. 368.

the Indies by the old route, he speaks of the decision arrived at to seek a new route northward by America.   He writes : " It is also decreed, that one Stephanus Gomez (who also himselfe a skillful Navigator) shall goe another way, where by betweene the Baccaloas, and Florida, long since our countries, he saith he will finde out a way to Cataia : one only shippe called a Caravel is furnished for him, *and he shall have no other thing in charge, then to search out wether any passage to the great Chan, from out the diuers windings, and vast compassing of this our Ocean, were to be found*" (dec. VI, chap. X).   Peter Martyr [1] thus speaks of the return of Gomez: " Now I come to Stephanus Gomez, who as I haue already sayd in the end of that booke presented to your Holinesse [Pope Clement VII,] beginning (before that) was sent with one Caravel to seeke another Straight betwene the land of Florida and the Bachalaos sufficiently known, and frequented.   He neither finding the straight, nor Gaitaia which he promised, returned backe within tenn monethes after his departure.   I always thought and presupposed this good man's imaginations were vayn and friuolous.   Yet wanted he no suffrages and voyces in

---

[1] Pope Leo was so much pleased with the narrations of Martyr that he used to sit up late at night reading them to his sister and the cardinals.

his fauor and defence. Notwithstanding he found
pleasant and profitable countries, agreeable with
our Parallels, and degrees of the Pole." The writer
then refers to a matter which he had treated of very
extensively in *Decade* VII, chapter iii, saying : " Li-
centiatus Aiglionus [Ayllon] also a Senator in
Hispaniola by his freindes, familiars travailed
& passed the *same strange shores to y° North of
Hispaniola, Cuba, and the Incaian Islands* neere y°
Bachalaos,[1] & the countryes of Chicora, and Duraba
whereof I speake at large before. Where, after
the declaration of the rites, and customs of the nations and the descriptions of *notable hauens and great
riuers,* groues of Holme, Oake, and Oliues, and
wild vines euery where there spreading in the woods,
they say, they founde also other trees of our countrey and that surely not in short Epitome, but con-
suming and expending great bundles of paper
therein. But what need haue we of these things
which are common with all the people of Europe ?
to the South, to the South [sic] for the great and
exceeding riches of the Æqunoctiall they that seek
riches must not go vnto the cold, and frosen north."

The full account of this voyage does not mention what was done at the northern part, near

---

[1] Cabot appears to have found this Basque word in use among
the natives, which, if true, proves that the Biscay fishermen had
anticipated the voyage of Columbus.

the " Bachaloas," by which was meant the country
above the forty-fourth parallel.   It is therefore to
be regretted that Peter Martyr did not think it
worth while to give the contents of those great bundles of paper.   These regions he had already remarked were " long since our countries. "

One story is related of Gomez's return (D. VIII, cx),
thought very laughable.   He tells the pope : "In
this adventure your Holinesse shall heare a pleasant & conceited puffe of winde arising, able to pro-
cure laughter.   This Stephanus Gomez hauing
attained none of those things which wee thought he
should haue found, lest he should returne empty,
contrary to the laws set down by vs, that no man
should offer violence to any nation, fraighted his
shipp with people of both sexes, taken from certaine innocent halfe naked nations, who contented
themselues in cottages insteede of houses.   And
when he came into the hauen Clunia, from whence
he set sayle, a certaine man hearing of the arri-
ual of his shippe, and that hee had brought Esclavos that is to say slaues, seekinge no further, came
postinge vnto us, with pantinge & breathless spirit
sayinge, that Stephanus Gomez bringeth his shippe
laden with cloues and precious stones; and
thought thereby to have received some rich present, or reward.   They who favored the matter,
attentiue to this manns foolish and idle report,

wearied the whole Court with exceedinge great applause, cuttinge of the worde by Aphæresis, proclayminge, that for Esclavos, hee had brought Clauos (for the Spanish tongue calleth slaves Esclavos, and cloues Clauos) but after the Court vnderstoode that the tale was transformed from Cloues to slaves, they break foorth into a great laughter, to the shame and blushinge of the fauorers who shouted for joy. If they hadd learned that the influence of the heauens could be nowhere infused into terestiall matters prepared to receiue that aromaticall spirit, saue from the Æquinoctiall Sunne, or next vnto it, they would have knowne, that in the space tenn moneths (wherein hee performed his voyage) aromaticall Cloues could not bee founde."

Gomez appears to have done his work quite thoroughly. In the course of the voyage he drew up a map, the outlines of which were afterwards embodied in the planisphere made by Ribero, now preserved in the British Museum. At a congress held at Badajos after the voyage of Gomez, where the most distinguished geographers of Spain and Portugal met to settle the disputes arising out of Pope Alexander's grant, the outlines of America were fixed for the first time from the discoveries of both nations.[1]

---

[1] See *Asher's Henry Hudson the Navigator*, p. xci Asher complains that Gomez's discoveries were so poorly put upon paper

The explorations of Gomez appear to have been the most thorough in latitude forty and forty-one. Oviedo had his reports, and gives among his descriptions the following statements:

"From Cape St. John to Cape or Promontory of the Sands, in 38° 20' are thirty leagues North Northeast; thence other 30 leagues North is Cape Santago in 39° 30'; thence the coast turns South-west 20 leagues to bay St. Chripstabel in 39°. From that bend made by the land the coast turns northward, passing said Bay 30 leagues to *Rio St. Antonio* in 41°, which is north and south with said bay." (*Hist. Mag.*, 1866, p. 369).

A careful comparison of all these accounts will persuade the reader that by the bay of St. Chripstabel is meant the lower bay of New York in connection with Raritan bay, and that Rio St. Antonio is the Hudson river. The latitudes are sufficiently exact for those times, but what is more noticeable is the fact stated, that this river lay north and south with the bay, which cannot be affirmed of any other river of note in this locality. In Ribero's map,[1] the whole country from

by Ribero. Yet we must remember that this was done at a time when map-making was in its infancy, and scientific accuracy was not always expected.

[1] The following, in relation to the early cartography of America, may here prove appropriate. Juan de la Cosa, otherwise known

New Jersey to Rhode Island is called *the land of Estevan Gomez,* while the land southward is called the *land of D'Ayllon.* Sprengel unites with Asher in demonstrating the discovery of the Hudson by Gomez. Asher thinks that the Spaniards who came to the coast after Gomez, also sometimes

as Juan Viscuyno, was a Biscayan. This person, accompanied Columbus on his second voyage to America, and took part in five expeditions, two of which he commanded. Bernardo de Ibarra says "that he saw and heard the Admiral [Columbus] complain of Juan de la Cosa, saying, that because he had brought him to these parts for the first time, and as a man of ability had taught him navigation, he went around saying that he knew more than himself." (*Notes on Columbus,* privately printed, New York, 1866, p. 38) Peter Martyr also says, speaking of the early maps : " Of all other, they most esteem them of Johannes de la Cossa, the companion of Fogeda (whom we sayde to be slayne of the people of Caramaivi in the hauen of Carthago) and another expert pilote called Andreas Moralis, had set forth." (*Dec.,* ii, cap. x.) These testimonies show that his reputation was deserved. In 1507 he received a pension of 50,000 maravedis for his services to the king. In 1507 he was appointed mayor of Uraba, and two years later, attending the expedition of Ojeda, at Darien, he lost his life, being slain by an Indian.

In 1832, Humboldt found his *Mappamundi* in the library of Walcknaer. This map was sold at auction in Paris for 4,020 francs. Perhaps it was the identical map that Petyr Martyr found in the study of Bishop Fonseca when he went to consult him in 1514, on the subject of newly found territories Beecher, in his *Landfall of Columbus,* p. xiv, says it is an "old document not worthy to be called a chart ;" but Humboldt testifies that it is the most important map known concerning the earliest history of the geography of the new world. Santarem and Lelewel coincide with this opinion. The map covers more than fifteen square feet of surface. The inscription is as follows :

called the river by his name, *Rio de Gamez*, as some also styled a river on the coast of Maine, instead of Rio St. Anthony. Asher informs us that the Hudson is thus called in the Spanish *routiers* made at the time for the use of those timid sailors who, even down to the seventeenth century, were ac-

---

Juan de la Cosa la fizo en el puerto de Sta Maria en año do 1500.

Above the inscription is a figure of St. Columbus, carrying the infant Christ through the sea, holding a globe, surmounted with a cross, in his right hand. A portion of the map in outline is given in *Lelewel's Collection of Ancient Maps*. Also in *Humboldt's Examen Critique*, vol. v; in *Ghillany's Behaim*; and in *Raman de la Sagra*.

The oldest printed map which contains the new world is the *Vniversailor Cognoti Orbit* of John Ruysch, which appeared in the edition of Ptolemy printed at Venice in 1508. The part upon which the western continent appears is given in *Ghillany's Behaim*.

The first person to suggest the name America as a proper name for the new continent was Martin Waldsee Muller, or Hylacomylus, who printed it in his *Globus Mundi* in 1507. A writer in a German review, in the course of an examination of Kunstmann's maps of America, declared that he had seen the name on an old map attached to a work by the Pole, John de Stobnicza, which appeared in 1512. But a careful examination reveals no such map, and the probability is that the reviewer in question was in error. (*Archeologia* of the London antiquaries, vol. xl).

A copy of a hitherto unknown map has, however, been discovered in the queen's library at Windsor Castle, and Mr. R. T. Major, the accomplished author of *Prince Henry the Navigator*, has exercised his ingenuity in providing a date for it. He claims these points for this map: namely. that it is the earliest map to indicate the severance of America from Asia, of Cuba from Japan, and the first to represent the southern continent.

customed to skirt the coast, instead of steering boldly
in a direct course for desired ports in the West Indies.
The mouth of the Hudson — Rio de Gamez — was
one of their stations, as was the case with the island
of Nantucket, called by the *routiers* Juan Luis or
Juan Fernandez.[1]

In this map Cuba and the Baccalloas appear as islands, and
the name America is given to the southern continent. Mr.
Major fixes the date of this map at 1513–14, for this reason,
among others, that it seems to indicate Balboa's discovery of the
Pacific. He attributes the authorship to no less a person than
that great genius Leonardi DaVinci ; and it must be confessed
that he sustains his positions with no little candor and ability.
But when we come to the year 1520 we have the word America in
a map whose age no one can dispute. This is the *Mappamundi* of
Appianus, which is given in the work of John Camertis.

One of the most interesting of the early maps is that of Ribero,
which bears the date of 1527, and gives the results of both Spanish and Portuguese explorations down to that date. A section of
this invaluable map is given in the work of the unfortunate
Lelewel. It is of especial interest in connection with the present
work, for the reason that it performs an important part in esta-
blishing the discovery of the Hudson by Gomez in 1525. Other
ancient and highly interesting maps relating to America will be
found in the collections of Kunstmann, and Jomard. The map
of Antonio Zeni is referred to elsewhere.

[1] In answer to a letter of inquiry, Dr. Asher writes to me,
under date of Heidelberg, Feb. 24, 1869, that the *routiers*
referred to are in the British Museum. In this connection I
may state that the old maps, which I have consulted, invariably
call the Hudson, Rio St. Antonio, and never Rio de Gamez, as
stated to be the case in the above mentioned *routiers*. On the
other hand the river of Gomez is always represented in the
latitude of the Penobscot, to which Gomez himself possibly
gave his name.

From all the foregoing testimony it must be clear to unprejudiced minds that, whoever may claim the honor of first discovering the River of St. Anthony, Henry Hudson can claim no part in it. Verrazano, Estevan Gomez, and the Dutch of 1598 all rise up to claim a long priority. Thus the old Labadist tradition takes life and meaning.

And such a result seemed long ago to have been anticipated and feared by the friends of Hudson who have, at times, caught a glimpse of the truth. The statement of Wassanaar who (*N. Y. Doc. Hist.*, vol. I, 35) speaks of the river of St. Anthony (for such we have a right to call it), as "the river called, first *Rio de Montagnes*, now the River *Mauritius*, lying in 40½ degrees," seems to have troubled Benson, like some handwriting on the wall, cancelling Hudson's claim. Still he was of good courage and inclined to be fair. Yet, notwithstanding the river was called River of the *Mountains*, he tells us that the early explorers, whoever they may have been, probably did not approach nearer than the Narrows.[1] It

[1] Benson quoted Van Der Donck who says : "There are some who maintain that the Spaniards were in this country many years before, but, finding it so cold, left it ; but I could never so understand it." But the Labadists so understood it, and even Petrus Stuyvesant, the Dutch governor, favored the French. Benson hesitates to sanction Van Der Donck, and says, " He was a Dutchman, and doubtless penned the passage, in asseveration of their

would, in the absence of all testimony to the contrary, appeared quite as reasonable to have concluded that they sailed up the Hudson, for when it is
once fairly entered, the name given by Wassanaar,
who was never in this country, and obtained it
abroad, appears every way appropriate. Indeed,
no one can say that Verrazano himself did not give
this name its European reputation. For in his letter
he well nigh brings out the idea, when he speaks of
the stream as a river of, or among, the *steep hills*.

According to our best knowledge, if we concede
the voyage of Verrazano, that navigator first
found [1] this grand river (*Grandissima riviera*), and
Estevan Gomez *named* it. They were separated
from one another by scarcely a year's time, and
neither appears to have had any knowledge at the
time of what the other had done.

---

title to the river as the first discoverers of it. He also says:
"I cannot forbear from the conjecture that they [the Spaniards]
approached so near as distinctly to discern the opening, the
Narrows, and concluding it to be the entrance to a river, and
Nevesinck and Staten Island being the only land on the coast
apparently *mountainous*, thence the name *River of the Mountains*." *N. Y. Hist. Coll.*, N. S., vol. II, p. 90. My own view,
after carefully consulting the map of Ribero and others, is that
the name River of the Mountains may have been first applied to
a river, east of Mount Desert, Maine, and afterwards transferred
to the Hudson.

[1] One well known and accomplished writer says that Verrazano simply "looked into the harbor of New York." This, however, is not the way that navigator states it.

What Verrazano accomplished at the River of the Steep Hills we are perfectly assured of, but how far Gomez ascended the so-called *Rio St. Antonio* [1] we are unable to say. Yet when we consider that his special aim was to search for some strait that might carry him to the Indies, it is not at all likely that he would have neglected to ascertain whither this broad opening led.

There is another point that has been claimed for Hudson which it will prove interesting to examine. One writer tells us that Hudson, by noting the singular amelioration of the climate, originated the great idea of an open polar sea," and refers to Mr. Murphy's monograph on Hudson as first bringing forward this fact. But Mr. Murphy simply says (p. 12) that after his second voyage he became known "because he had reached, as was supposed, that tempting region of Arctic exploration, the open Polar sea." De Veer's account of the Dutch expedition of 1594, which account (p. 41) was

---

[1] Benson, in his *Memoirs* says, that " the promontory in the Highlands [is] called *Antonie's Noze*, after *Antonie De Hooge*, secretary of the colony of Rensselaerwyck." He gives no authority for the opinion. The Labadist brethren called it *Antonis neus* (*L. I. Hist. Coll.* vol. I, p. 330) and say that all the headlands, " bear the names that were originally given to them," and this because it has the form of a man's nose. All the Dutch Anthonies appear to have claimed it in turn; but what if it should finally appear that it was named by the Spaniards, who gave the whole river into the charge of St. Anthony ?

probably written by Barentz, argues substantially
in favor of an open sea.   It is distinctly declared
that " the nearness of the pole was not the cause of
the great colde we felt."

The writer says that it is " as hot under $23\frac{1}{2}°$
as under the line," and asks " what wonder then
should it bee that about the North Pole also and
as many degrees on both sides of it should not bee
colder then right under the Pole."   He afterwards
continues, "Thus much will I say, that though we
held not our direct pretended course to North-east,
that therefore it is to bee iuged that the colde
would have let no one pass through that way, for
it was not the Sea, nor the nearnesse unto the
Pole, but the ice about the [main] land that let
and hindered vs (as I sayd before) for that as soon
as we made *from* the land, and put more into the
Sea, although it was much further northward, pre-
sently we felt more warmth; and in that opinion
our pilote William Barentz died."

In the account of the voyage of 1595 the writer
argues against the old idea "y^t 350 miles at least
of the North Pole on both sides are not to be sailed,
which appeareth not to be true, for that the White
sea and farther northward is now sayled."   The
writer also says that it is by the farre colder there
[on the main] then it is a greate deal nearer the
pole in the large seas."   His theory was that the

ice came down the rivers of northern Europe and accumulated on the coast, while the water to the northward was open, affording a route to China. Hence the expedition of 1595 boldly tried to push north of Nova Zembla, instead of seeking to go as at first between that island and the main. If any navigator of that period is entitled to be considered the originator of the theory of an open polar sea, that person was Barentz, the pilot of the first three expeditions, with which Hudson had no connection. The same view is supported by the letter of President Jeanin, written from the Hague, January 21, 1609, to Henry IV, and given by Asher in his *Henry Hudson the Navigator* (p. 244). In this letter (p. 245) he says " an English pilot, who has twice sailed in search of a northern passage, has been called to Amsterdam by the East India Company, to tell them what he had found, and whether he hoped to discover that passage. They were well satisfied with his answer, and had thought they *might* succeed in the scheme." This does not even bear out the remark of Mr. Murphy before quoted, where he intimates that the Dutch had *supposed* Hudson had reached the open sea. Jeanin afterwards says, " Plancius maintains, according to the reasons of his science, and from the information given him, both by the Englishman (Hudson) and other pilots who have been engaged in the same navigation, that there must be in the northern ports a passage corresponding to the one found near the South pole by Magellan. One of these pilots has been there three [*thirteen*, i. e., 1594] years ago."

This pilot who preceded Hudson has already been alluded to, and his own language shows that it was he, and not Plancius, who worked out the idea of an open polar sea.[1] This claim for Hudson is therefore unsupported. Indeed it will be found impossible to erect a character of greatness for Henry Hudson. As already remarked his mind was cast in an ordinary mould, and possessed no elements of originality. He was a good copyist but hardly more.[2]

----

[1] I here use the popular language in regard to the Polar sea. In the year 1500, it is believed Columbus predicted the discovery of the North pole.

[2] Foster claimed that Hudson discovered Spitzbergen, having forgotten his own declaration, in another place, where he says " Hudson saw Spitzbergen in 1607, which had been discovered eleven years before by the Dutch." Barrow, speaking more to the point, says in his *Chronological History of Arctic Regions*, that " it deserves to be remarked that he was the first of northern navigators, and probably the first Englishman, who made observations on the inclination or dip of the needle." His observation made in his second voyage may be found in *Asher's Henry Hudson*, p. 25. If Barrow had said that Hudson was the first of a class of navigators to *record* the dip of the needle it would have been better. He certainly could not have been the first to notice the fact, unless all his predecessors were blind.

It only remains now to speak briefly of the translators of Ivar Bardsen's work.

First is William Barentz, or Barentsen, the distinguished explorer. Barentsen was a Dutch navigator, who made three voyages for the purpose of reaching China by north-east sea. His first attempt was in 1594, and the second in 1595, and the third the following year. The account of these expeditions, originally written in Dutch, are given by Purchas,[1] with some brief memoranda by Barentsen himself. Purchas says that he found the sailing directions of Bardsen among Hakluyt's papers in Barentsen's own hand. Hakluyt says that it was loaned to him, by Peter Plancius, in Amsterdam, March 27, 1609. It does not appear that Barentsen ever made use of the directions. The date of his death I do not find. The version of Bardsen which fell into his hands is, in the opinion of Prof. Rafn and others, the best extant.

Jodicus Hondius, who is mentioned as possessing the first translation, was born at Wackene, in Flanders, in the year 1563. In his eighth year he began to draw and engrave on steel and ivory, afterwards becoming distinguished as a scientific map engraver. During the siege of Antwerp, he was employed by the Duke of Parma in exe-

[1] See *Purchas his Pilgrimes*, vol. III, pp. 473, 518.

cuting some statues in bronze. He was recommended by the duke to visit Italy to study art, but declined the opening. Afterwards he went to England, but eventually settled in Amsterdam, where he died in 1611. His son succeeded him in his profession. Among the portraits which he engraved are those of Queen Elizabeth, Sir Francis Drake and Thomas Cavendish.

Of William Stere, merchant, who translated Barentsen's version into English, nothing of particular interest is known.

Peter Plancius was a minister of the reformed faith in Amsterdam. Born in Drenoutre, Flanders, in 1552, he pursued his studies in England and Germany. He was ordained to the ministry in 1577, and preached in various parts of Brabant. His books were publicly burnt at Ypres. Afterwards becoming minister of the Reformed Church at Brussels he officiated there for a period of six years. On the capture of that place by the Duke of Parma, he escaped into Holland, disguised as a soldier, and settled over the church in Amsterdam, where he proved a determined opponent of the doctrines of Luther and Arminius. He sat in the synod of Dort in the year 1618, and was a member of the committee on the translation of the Old Testament. He died in the city of his adoption May 25, 1622, aged seventy years. He gave directions concerning his burial, in accordance with which his remains were interred in the south church-yard of Amsterdam.

The Rev. Peter Plancius, in common with many of his Belgian countrymen, did much to make Holland the centre of geographical knowledge. Asher says that Plancius was one of the most eminent of the geographical students, and, like the late Sir John Barrow, was universally known for his interest in the search for a northern route for China, a subject which he had discussed with Hudson himself,[1] taking an active interest in all the voyages of the distinguished navigator. It is also said that he opened a school for the study of navigation, with especial reference to new routes to China. He afterwards had an interest in a venture to the Hudson river. It must be conceded that his influence upon the whole subject of discovery was highly beneficial.

Since the foregoing was put in type, the new volume of the Maine Historical Society, edited by Dr. Kohl, of Bremen, has come to hand. Concerning the voyage of Kolnus, he says on page 114:

---

[1] See Asher's *Henry Hudson*, p. xlvi.

"Many have repeated this report without finding any other authority for it than Gomara and Wytfliet. But the Danish and Norwegian writers upon this subject consider that voyage as altogether apocryphal, and say, that their old northern historians and documents do not contain the slightest mention of such an expedition. Moreover, they think that if it was made at all, it could have been nothing more than an attempt to find out again the lost Old Greenland, and not to make new discoveries in the distant west. The learned Polish geographer, Lelewel, though inclined, from a patriotic motive, to make a great deal of the undertaking, ascribed to his countrymen, has found no Polish authority whatever."

To these statements no weight need be attached, for a variety of reasons.

The sweeping declaration that Danish and Norwegian writers consider "that voyage as altogether apocryphal," is rested on the opinion of Finn Magnusen, expressed in *Grönland's Historiske Mindesmærker* (vol. III, p. 630), and in his *Essay on the Ancient Trading Voyages from England to Iceland*. As regards the fact that the "old northern historians and documents do not contain the slightest mention of such an expedition," it may be observed: First. That we have no proof that the state archives of Denmark, at the period referred to, were of that perfect and comprehensive character which would insure the record of every such event. Second. That if they were thus perfect, originally, we have no proof that the collections remain unimpaired. Third. We are not positive that these or other archives do *not* contain some reference to this voyage. Hakluyt lamented that there was no account of the ships or the persons engaged in the English expedition of John Rut to America, in the year 1527, and his regrets were echoed by the principal writers who followed, down to the time of Dr. Lardner and the *Edinburgh Cabinet* who accompanied the expression of regret with others that savored of indignation. Yet all the while the evidence existed, and might have been read at the time even in Purchas. And if so many writers could overlook, for so long a period, the testimony in regard to Rut, it is not at all unreasonable to suppose that the full history of Skolnus may still be lying in some neglected corner. At least the multitude of similar cases that might be cited should inspire us with a large degree of caution.

Gomara, in 1553, did not bring forward John Skolnus without reason. Michael Lok in 1582, appears to have had entire confidence in his voyage; while Wytfliet had quite full information of the expedition in 1597. It is of course, to be lamented that he made no mention of his authority.

Still the Swedish historian Pontanus followed him without hesitation. On far less authority, Dr. Kohl accepts the voyage of Dénys of Honfleur, set down for 1506.

As to Dr. Kohl's remark that the northern historians confine the object of Kolnus's voyage to a search for Old Greenland, we have only to say that no one attributed to it a larger aim. Yet, even with that purpose in view, it would have been just as easy for him to have discovered Labrador in 1476, as for Biarne when, on a similar voyage, in 985, to discover the continent of America.

The insinuation that Lelewel felt inclined to magnify this " undertaking ascribed to his countrymen," has no foundation in the Polish writer's simple and disinterested account. Besides the voyage was never ascribed " to his countrymen." It was uniformly ascribed to Denmark, Kolnus being merely the pilot.

It is a sufficient reply to the statements that he "found no Polish authority whatever" for this voyage, to say that Lelewel did not *look* for any Polish authority (see his *Geographie Du Moyen Age*, vol. II, p. 106).

Laying aside all national prejudices, and viewing the alleged voyage of Kolnus in all its bearings, it, on the whole, appears sufficiently reasonable to be classed among authentic voyages. It might

well have been forgotten by the people of Denmark
(if it *was* forgotten) at a time when the nation was
constantly threatened by calamity. The great ob-
jection to the voyage of Kolnus is, very likely,
based upon that unfortunate hallucination which
still sways so many minds, and leads not a few historical students to look upon pre-Columbian voyages
from the European Continent, as a sort of libel upon
the name of that illustrious navigator whose real
merits do not always enter into estimates of
his character, or dignify traditional admiration.
Happily, however, the world moves; and when ill-
founded prejudice has passed away, the opponent
of pre-Columbian voyages will find that he has been
shorn of his most powerful argument.

SAILING DIRECTIONS.

A Treatise of IVER BOTY *a Gronlander, translated out of the* Norsh *Language into High* Dutch, *in the yeere* 1560. *And after out of High* Dutch, *into Low* Dutch, *by* WILLIAM BARENTSON *of Amsterdam, who was chiefe Pilot aforesaid.* The *same Copie in High* Dutch *is in the hands of* IODOCVS HONDIVS, *which I haue seene. And this was translated out of Low* Dutch *by* Master WILLIAM STERE, *Marchent, in the yeere* 1608, *for the use of me* HENRIE HUDSON. WILLIAM BARENTSONS *Booke is in the hands of Master* PETER PLANTIVS, *who lent the same to me.*

N *primis*, it is reported by men of Wisedome and Vnderstanding borne in *Gronland*, That from *Stad*[1] in *Norway* to the East part of Island, called Hornnesse,[2] is seven dayes sayling right West.

Item, men shall know, that betweene *Island* and

---

[1] The words in the old Danish text given by Rafn is also *Stad*, a city or town. Bergen is the place referred to.

[2] *Horn-nesse* simply means Horn-*Cape*, the term *nesse* or *ness* having the same signification wherever it occurs.

Gronland, lyeth a Risse [1] called *Gombornse-skare.* [2]
There they were wont to have their passage for

[1] *Risse,* the old preterite of the verb *rise,* used by Ben
Jonson, but now obsolete. It seems to mean a place where the
ocean's bed is lifted up above the water. The term does not
occur in the Danish.

[2] *Gombornse-skare,* i. e., Gunnbiorn's *schier* or *rock.* Here
the locality of these famous rocks is left undecided, but the Danish version says that they lay " half way " between Iceland and
Greenland. Torfæus says that these rocks were six sea miles
from *Geirfuglesker* off Reikiavik, and twelve miles south of Garda
in Greenland ; yet it is possible that they may have been sunk
in some of the many convulsions that have happened in and
near Iceland. The *Landanama,* or Icelandic Dooms-day book,
has some account of their original discovery by Gunnbiorn, Ulf
Krage's son, in the year A. D. 876. In the year 970, Snæbiorn
and a company of adventurers sailed from Iceland to these rocks
where they spent the winter. The account says that :

" Snæbiorn also took Thorod from Thingness, his step-father
and his five sons, and Rolf took Stærbiorn. The last named re-
cited the following verse, after he had a dream :

> Both ours
> dead I see ;
> all empty
> in Northwestern Sea ;
> cold weather,
> great suffering,
> I expect
> Snæbiorn's death.

They sought Gunnbiorn's Rocks and found land. Snæbiorn
would not permit any one to go ashore in the night. Stærbiorn
landed notwithstanding, and found a purse with money in an
earth hole, and concealed it. Snæbiorn hit him with an axe so
that the purse fell down. They built a cabin to live in, and it
was all covered with snow. Thorkel Red's son, found that there
was water on a shelf that stood out of the cabin window. This

Gronland. But as they report there is Ice on the The long North bottome. same Risse, come out of the long North Bottome,[1] so

---

was in the month of Goe [about February.] They shoveled the snow away. Snæbiorn rigged the ship; Thorod and five of his party were in the hut, and Stærbiorn and several men of Rolf's party. Some hunted. Stærbiorn killed Thorod, but both he and Rolf killed Snæbiorn. Red's sons and all the rest were obliged to take the oath of allegiance to save their lives. They arrived on their return at Helgeland, Norway, and later at Vadil in Iceland." See *Pre-Columbian Discovery*, pp. 11 – 15.

This is about all the positive history connected with Gunnbiorn's Rocks; yet it may be interesting to state what Graah says on the subject in his account of the boat voyage along the eastern shore of Greenland. When in latitude about 65° 35′ a heavy gale set in which drove some ice out to sea, "by which means," he says "I got sight of two, or perhaps, three large islands in that direction, distant from forty to fifty miles. These are, probably, the islands between which Danel states that he passed in the year 1652, though they lie somewhat nearer the main land, than, according to his account, they ought. It is likewise in all likelihood, these same islands that the ancients called Gunbiörn's Skerries, and which, they state, lay midway between Iceland and Greenland, that is to say (according to my interpretation of the words) midway between Iceland and the Bygd in Greenland, which, in fact, they do exactly, if, by the Bygd we are to understand the present district of Julian's Hope, and keep in mind, that, in the early period of the Greenland colonization, those sailing for the colony did not shape a course direct S. W. from Iceland, but first steered west till they made the land and then proceeded south along the shore." — *Graah's Expedition*, p. 100.

[1] *North Bottome.* The Danish is *Botnen*, meaning the Northern ocean, from whence, since the times of Eric the Red and Snæbiorn, the ice has been drifting more freely than before. It now crowds upon the eastern coast with such force that it is almost impossible to make a boat voyage along the shore except at certain brief and favorable seasons.

that we cannot use the same old Passage as they thinke.[1]

Item, from Long-nesse [2] on the East side of *Island* to the aboue said *Horn-nesse*,[3] is two dayes sayle to the *Brim-stone* Mount.[4]

---

[1] This paragraph, it must be observed, is not so full as in Rafn's Danish version, which also says that the distance from Snæfellsness to Greenland is " two days' and two nights' sail." Graah says of the Danish version : " Eggers has, in my opinion, satisfactorily proved, that the old writers have committed an error here in stating the distance to be a *two* days' sail to the west, and that in the place of *two* we should read *four*. Worms-kiold, on the other hand, who combats Eggers's statements, holds, that the error lies in the punctuation of the passage. I, for my part, believe both are right ; and while I read with Eggers *four* days '; instead of two, I place, with Wormskiold, a comma after the words ' *er kortest til Grönland*,' [shortest to Greenland] from which correction it results, that the distance from Iceland to *Gunbiorn's Skerries* was four days sail to the west, and Gunbiorn's Skerries being expressly stated to be exactly half way between Iceland and Greenland, that is, between Iceland and *the Bygd*, the distance between the latter, was eight days' sail " (p. 100, *n.*).

[2] The Danish says that *Long-nesse*, or *Langeness*, is on the *north-east* side of Iceland, which is the more exact statement, as will be seen by consulting a good Icelandic map.

[3] This is what is now known as the East Horn, or Cape.

[4] In the Danish version we read *till* [to] *Svalbarde* [in] *Haff's-botnen*. *Svalbarde* indicates a *frozen shore*, and *Haffsbotnen*, a sea-bay. Rafn calls attention to the original observation on this point in the *Saga* of Olaf Tryggvesson, in *Sturleson's Heim-skringla*. See *Rafn's Antiquitates Americanæ*, p. 303, n. ; and *Laing's Heimskringla*. The Brimstone mount referred to is Hecla. Purchas says that in the last voyage of Hudson " they passed Island, and saw Mount Hecla cast out fire, a noted signe of foule weather towards ; others conceive themselves and de-

Item, if you goe from *Bergen* in *Norway*, the course is right West, till you bee South of *Roke-nesse*[1] in *Island:* and distant from it thirteene[2] miles or leagues. And with this course you shall come vnder that high Land that lyeth in the East part of *Groneland*, and is called *Swaster*.[3] A day before you come there, you shall have sight of a high Mount, called *Huit-sarke:*[4] and between *Whit-sarke* and *Groneland*[5] lyeth a headland called *Her-noldus Hooke;*[6] and thereby lyeth an Hauen, where

Swaster.

Whit-sarke.

Hernoldus Hooke.

ceiue others with I know not what purgatorie fables hereof confuted by Arngrim Jonas, an Islander, who reproueth this and many other dreams related by authors, saying that from the year 1558 to 1592 it never cast forth any flames." (*Asher*, p. 140; *Purchas*, III, p. 654).

[1] Reikianess, the cape near the capital of Iceland, at the south-west extremity.

[2] The Danish version says *twelve*. Olaf Trygvesson's *Saga* also says *twelve*. These twelve miles equalled about seventy or eighty common miles.

[3] The Danish for *Swalster* is *Hvarf*, which means a place of turning, by which is understood the promontory some distance northward from the south point of Greenland.

[4] In the original *Huidserk*, which means *white shirt*, the jokul at the extremity of Greenland.

[5] By Groneland is meant that port for which the Icelanders usually sailed, and called the East *Bygd*, though situated on the west coast, in the modern district of Julian's Hope.

[6] *Hernoldus Hooke*, is simply Heriulfsness, a little to the west of *Huidserk*. In this connection we must notice the corresponding directions of the *Landanama Bok*, which agree with the directions laid down in this paragraph: "From the houses [Bergen] in Norway, you must sail steadily to the west to Hvarf in Greenland, passing north of the Shetland [islands],

Sound Hauen in *Gronland.*

the Norway Merchant Ships were wont to come:
and it is called *Sound Hauen*.[1]

Item, if a man will sayle from ·Island to Gronland hee shall set his course to *Snofnesse*,[2] which is
by West *Rokenesse*[3] thirteene[4] miles or leagues right
West one day and night's[5] sayling, and after South-
west to shun the Ice,[6] that lyeth on *Gombornse-
skare;* and after that one day and night North-

so that the horizon is seen between the mountains, if the weather
is clear, but South of the Faroe Island, so that the horizon is seen
between the mountains, and south of Iceland, so that you fall
in with birds and whales." The region of whales is situated
about where Ivar Bardson puts it, twelve Icelandic sea miles,
or nearly eighty ordinary miles from the coast. Graah, after
summing up the whole matter, says at the conclusion, " I am very
confident that a seaman of the present day, if, without compass,
chart or quadrant, he was directed to sail from Bergen to Cape
Farewell, would follow the exact course laid down in the *Landanama Book.*" See *Graah*, p. 157. This book was begun by
Frode, called the Wise, about the year 1100, and was finished
before the death of Erlandson in 1334. See *Pre-Columbian
Discovery*, p. xxiii, n. It is interesting to know that Henry
Hudson went forth on his voyage of 1609 with these ancient
directions, which might have proved an invaluable guide.

[1] *Sound Hauen, i. e.,* Sand Haven.

[2] Snæfellsness.

[3] Reikianess.

[4] The Danish again differs from this translation. putting the distance at *twelve* miles.

[5] The original says, *een Dagh och een Natt;* on which Rafn
remarks: *forsitan II dagr duobus nyethemerus.*

[6] That fine old Icelandic work called the *Royal Mirror* (*Spe-
culum Regale*), speaking of the ice, says : " This ice lies more
in the direction of north and north-east than south, south-west,

west. So shall he with this course fall right with the aboue sayed *Swaster*, which is high Land, under which lyeth the aforesayd Head-land, called *Hernoldus Hooke*, and the *Sound Hauen*.

Item, the *Easter*[1] Dorpe[2] of *Groneland* lyeth East from *Hernoldus Hooke*, but neere it, and is called *Skagen* Ford[3] and is a great village. *Skagen Ford.*

Item, from *Skagen* Ford, East, lyeth a Hauen called *Beare* Ford,[4] it is not dwelt in. In the mouth thereof lyeth a Risse, so that great ships cannot harbour in it. *Beare Ford.*

Item, there is great abundance of Whales: and there is great Fishing for the killing of them there: but not without the Bishops consent, which keepeth the same for the benefit of the Cathedrall A great fishing for Whales.

----

and west; for which reason, he that would reach the land must sail around it, till he passes all the ice, and then sail in for the land." It says that it has "often chanced that those sailing for this land have held in too soon, and have thus got caught in the ice, where some have been lost, and others have with much exertion escaped; and the method they have usually adopted was to haul their boats upon the ice, and make the best of their way with them to the shore, abandoning their ships and all their goods on board of them to destruction. Some have managed to live on the ice in this way four or five days, others even a longer time." See *Rafn's Antiquitates Americanæ*, p. 305, n.; *Graah*, p. 159.

[1] *Easter*, or east.
[2] *Dorpe*, the original is *bygd*, a district.
[3] *Skagenford*, that is *Skagafiord*, from *Skagefjord*.
[4] *Beare ford*, from *Bere fjord*, the fiord of bears.

church.   In the Hauen there is a *Swalth:*[1] and when the Tide doth runne out, all the Whales doe runne into the sayd *Swalth.*

A great Swalth.

Item, East of *Beare* Ford, lyeth another Hauen called *Allabong* Sound:[2] and it is at the mouth narrow, but farther in, very wide: the length whereof is such, that the end thereof is not yet knowne.   There runneth no Streame.   It lyeth full of little Isles.   Fowle and Oxen are there com-

Allabong Sound.

Store of oxen.

---

[1] Swalth, eddy, or whirlpool.   In such places the smaller fish usually resort to play or seek their food, and hither they are always followed by the whales.

[2] *Allabong Sound.*   It is with difficulty that we recognize the phrase in Purchas.   The old Danish is *Ollumlengri*, which Rafn translates, *Omnium-longissimus*, the longest (fiord) of all. Those who in old times supposed that the East *Bygd* lay upon the east coast of Greenland located it in latitude 70°, making it identical with Scoresby's Sound, which place was discovered by the Dane, Volgvard Boou, in 1769.   In the very old maps of Greenland, the sound was represented as narrow, and extending nearly across Greenland, which it almost reduced to an island. We know now that this place was certainly on the west coast. Besides, Scoresby's Sound, as Graah observes, has strong currents, and *no* isles, birds or eggs ; while its mouth, instead of being narrow, is four or five times wider than any other fiord in Greenland of which we have any knowledge.   There are nevertheless places that correspond to *Ollum-leingri* in the southern tracts of Greenland.   At Illoa Arctander saw green fields, and in two of the entrances to this fiord there are numerous small isles and holms.   There are also many birds and eggs, though the current is rapid.   Yet the current may have been created by one of those changes constantly occurring, while in the day of Bardson the ice-blinks may have cut off approach and rendered it impossible to reach the end.

mon : and it is playne Land on both Sides, growne
ouer with greene grasse.

Item, East from the Icie Mountayne, lyeth an
Hauen *Fendebother ;* [1] so named, because in Saint
Olaues time there was a Ship cast away, as the
Speach hath been in *Groneland ;* In which Ship was
drowned one of Saint Olaues men, with others : and
those that were saued did burie those that were
drowned, and on their Graues did set great stone
Crosses, which we see at this day.

Item, from somewhat more East toward the Icie
Mountayne lyeth a high Land, called *Corse Hought,* [2]
vpon which they hunt white Beares, but not without the Bishops leaue, for it belongeth to the Cathedrall church. And from thence more easterly,
men see nothing but Ice and Snow, both by land
and Water.

Now we shall return again to *Hernoldus Hooke,*
where we first began to come to the first Town

The Icie Mount-ayne.
The Hauen of Fende-bother.

Corse Hought.
An hunt-ing of White Beares. More East-erly all Desert.

The towns from Her-noldus Hooke.

---

[1] *Fendebother.* The original is *Finsbuder.* The notes of
Rafn throw no additional light on this passage. By referring
to the sagas which relate to Greenland, it will be found that
shipwrecks were of very frequent occurrence. The greater part
of Eric the Red's fleet was either driven back from Greenland
or lost.

[2] *Corse Hought.* The original is *Kaarsooe* or Cross Island.
Wormskiold, who advocated the exploded theory of a settlement on the east coast of Greenland, thought that this island was
Jan Mayen, sixty-five miles from the nearest point of Greenland, and eight hundred from what he thought was the East

that lyeth on the east side of *Hernoldus Hooke,*
called *Skagen* Ford: and so we will write the
names of all that lye on the West-side of the Ford
or Sound.

Item, West from *Hernoldus Hooke,* lyeth a Dorpe
called Kodosford,[1] and it is well built: and as you
sayle into the Sound, you shall see on the right
hand a great Sea and Marsh : and into this Sea runneth a great streame : and by the Marsh and Sea
standeth a great Church,[2] on which the Holy
Crosse is drawne, of colour white : it belongeth to

West-
ward.

The towne
of Godos-
ford.

A great
Church
with a
white
Cross on
it.

Bygd. In Zorgdrager's map there was a cross, yet it did not
indicate the name of the isle, but pointed to the graves of
seven Dutchmen who in 1643 attempted to winter there. We
may yet be able to identify this place in some of the fiords of
the west coast.

[1] *Kodosford,* from Ketilsfjord. Every chief settler who went
to Greenland appropriated some advantageous spot and gave it
his own name to mark his proprietorship. Thus we read that
" Among those who emigrated [A. D. 985-6] with Eric and established themselves, were Heriulf Heriulfsfiord, who took Heriulfsness, and abode in Heriulfsness, Ketil Ketilsfiord, Rafn
Rafnsfiord, Solvi Solvidale, Helgi Thorbrandson Alptafiord,
Thorbjornglora Siglefjord, Einar Einarsfiord, Hafgrim Haf-
grimsfiord and Vatnahver, Arnlaug Arnlaugsfiord : and other
men went to the west district."

This name *Ketil,* is probably that from which all the modern
forms have been derived. See Saga of Eric the Red in *Antiquitates Americanæ,* p. 15; and *Pre-Columbian Discovery,* p. 17.
The location of the fiord in question cannot now with certainty
be pointed out.

[2] The Danish calls it *Auroos Church.*

Enelnesse de Hokesong,[1] and the land to *Peters Wike*.[2]

Item, by *Peters Wike* lyeth a great Dorpe called *Wartsdale*,[3] by which lyeth a Water or Sea of twelue miles or leagues ouer: in which is much Fish. And to *Peters Wike* Church belongeth *Wartsdale* Bay or Towne, and the villages. *Peters Wike.* *Wartsdale* *Bay* in the *Norse* tongue sig-nifieth a *Towne.*

Item, neere this Bay or Towne, lyeth a Cloyster or Abbey,[4] in which are Canons Regular, it is dedicated to Saint *Olaves*, and Saint *Augustines* name. And to it belongeth all the Land to the Sea side, and towards the other side of the Cloyster. A Monasterie.

Item, next *Godosford*,[5] lyeth a ford called *Rompnes*

---

[1] Who this person was does not now appear. In the Danish version *Enelnesse de Hokesong* is not mentioned.

[2] *Peters Wike* (*Niigh*) or bay. The origin of this name is obscure.

[3] *Wartsdale* from *Vatnsdale*.

[4] The voyage of the Zeni brothers performed very near the end of the thirteenth century, gives an account of a monastery in Greenland; but the account is so poor that it leads us either to question the correctness of the narrative or to find some other location for the abbey. Besides it appears to describe what was seen on the east coast, where no monastery was ever built, and the writer confines himself almost entirely to a single point, as if he really knew nothing about Greenland. Yet this is not so. He simply lacked correct information on this point. Of the reality of the religious houses in Greenland at that early period there can be no doubt.

[5] Here Purchas's, or rather, Hudson's version, varies from the Danish, which says, " next to Ketilsfiord," instead of *Godosford*, which *may* mean *Gardafiord*.

A Nunne-
rie.

ford :[1] and there lyeth a Cloyster of Nuns of Saint *Benedict's* Order.

Item, this Cloyster to the bottome of the Sea and

Wegen Kerke.

to *Wegen Kerke*,[2] was Dedicated to Saint Olave [3] the King. In this Ford lye many small Isles. And to this Cloyster belongeth halfe the Ford and

Hot waters in Groene-land.

the Church. In this Sound are many Warm Waters.[4] In the Winter they are intollerable hot : but in the Summer more moderate; and many Bathing in them are cured of many diseases.

---

[1] *Rompnes ford* is *Rafnsfjord*, or the bay of Rafn, an early settler mentioned in a previous note.

[2] *Wegen Kerke*. The Danish is *Voge Kierche*.

[3] Saint Olaf Trygvesson, king of Norway at the close of the tenth and at the beginning of the eleventh century.

[4] These thermal springs are found in Greenland, as well as in Iceland, where they especially abound. Graah says of the Greenland springs : " On our way back we visited the hot springs at Ounartok. The western side of this island, which lies at the mouth of a firth of the same name, is lofty, rugged and almost totally naked, while the opposite side is low and clothed with the most luxuriant vegetation. It is on this side that the springs are situated, lying, all three of them, close by one another, at the N. E. corner of the island. Of these springs, the one nearest the sea is altogether insignificant : the temperature of its water was found to be 26° ; the second, a few paces from it forms a lake of about forty-eight feet in circuit, and the temperature of its water was 27° ; the third is still larger, being about seventy feet in circuit, and its water from 32° to 33½°, all of Reaumur. The depth of these pools nowhere exceeded a foot, and their bottom is composed of a soft, blueish clay, through which the warm water bubbled up at several places. The two large ones the Greenlanders have dammed up with stone, and make use of as bathing places. Near the middle of one, Are-

Item, betweene *Rompnes* and the next Sound, lyeth a great Garden called Vose,[1] belonging to the King.[2] There is also a costly Church dedicated to Saint Nicolas. This Church had the King before this. Neere it lyeth a Sea of Fresh water,[3] called —— in which is great abundance of Fish, without number. And when there falleth much Rayne, that the waters do rise therewith, and after fall againe, there remayneth vpon the Land much Fish drie.

Item, when you sail out of *Emestnes* Ford,[4] there lyeth an inlet, called *South-woders wike*:[5] and some-

(marginal notes: A place called Vose belonging to the King. Saint Nicholas Church. Emestnes Ford. Southwoders Wicke.*)*

tander found, in 1777, the remains of a small building, which he took to be from the time of the old colonists, and whose walls were then a foot and a half high. Every vestige of them has, however, vanished, and their place is occupied by the remains of an old Greenland hut. The water of these springs deposits a siliceous or calcareous sediment like Geyser and Strokr in Iceland. The Greenlanders state that it is much hotter in winter than in summer : but this opinion may proceed from the circumstance of the atmospheric air being much colder."—*Expedition*, p. 36.

[1] *Vose*, original *Foss*.

[2] The revenue derived by Denmark and Norway was not altogether inconsiderable.

[3] The Danish does not indicate that the water of this lake was fresh ; yet curiously enough this has been reported by others. Arctander says that at Kakartok he discovered on the top of a small hill a fresh-water lake, containing cod and halibut, and whose waters rose and fell. Arctander is positive, yet Graah says that he could neither find it nor learn anything about it from the natives. A man like Arctander certainly could not have altogether imagined this.

[4] *Emestnes fiord*, Danish, *Einersfjord*.

[5] *South-woders wike*, Danish *Thorvaldsvig*, the fiord or bay of Thorvald, one of the early settlers.

what higher in the same Sound, and on the same

Bloming. side, lyeth a little Cape called *Bloming:*[1] and be-

Gran- yond that lyeth another Inwike called *Granwike*,[2]
wicke.
Daleth and above that lyeth a Garden called *Daleth*,[3]
Garden.
which belongeth to the Cathedrall Church.   And

on the right hand as you sayle out of the same

A great Sound, lyeth a great Wood,[4] which pertayneth to
Wood.
the Church, where they feede all their Cattell,[5] as

---

[1] *Bloming*, the Danish is *Klüing.* On the significance of this name Rafn remarks : *Promontorium illud probabiliter abundarit aliquo argillæ, calcis aut limi genere, vel murorum constructioni vel terræ lætamini apto.—Antiquitates Americanæ,* p. 311 *n.*

[2] *Granwike.* Danish *Granerig.* Prof. Rafn remarks that this name has a variety of derivations. Among others he gives *Granerig (Grafarik) sinus fossarum vel Sepulchorum*, which would indicate that it was the Golgotha of Greenland." *Antiquitates Americanæ,* p. 311 *n.*

[3] *Daleth.* The word was suggested to the translator by *Daler*, from the Icelandic *Dale*, a common name for gardens in Iceland and Scandinavia.

[4] *Woods.* A great wood or forest in the mind of an Icelander need not amount to more than a patch of birches varying from one foot to ten feet high. In Iceland there was standing a short time since, one tree twenty-six feet high, which was regarded with wonder. Ivar Bardsen doubtless felt that the low birches and shrubs that are found in parts of Greenland merited the term applied.

[5] Cattle are frequently mentioned in the Sagas that describe Greenland. It is not likely that many were kept in the later period of the colonies. In modern times there has been nothing to prevent the people from keeping such animals, though it has been found better to substitute dogs for horses. Crantz says, that in "the year 1759, one of our missionaries brought three

Oxen, Kine and Horses: And to the Church pertayneth the Sound of *Emestnes* Ford. The high
Land lying off *Emestnes* Ford, is called *The Ray-
mos hayth :*[1] so called, because that on those Hills
doe runne many *Roe Deere,* or *Reyne Deer,*[2] which
they vse to Hunt, but not without the Bishops
leaue. And on this high Land is the best Stone
in all *Groneland.* They make thereof Pots, because fire cannot hurt it. And they make of the
same Stone Fattes,[3] or Cisterns, that will hold ten
or twelue Tunnes of water.

---

sheep with him from Denmark to New Herrnhuth. These have
so increased by bringing some two, some three lambs a year, that
they have been able to kill some every year since, to send some
to Lichtenfels, for a beginning there, and, after all, to winter
ten at present. We may judge how vastly sweet and nutritive
the grass is here, from the following tokens: that tho' three
lambs come from one ewe, they are larger, even in autumn,
than a sheep of a year old in Germany." He says that in the
summer they could pasture two hundred sheep around New
Herrnhuth; and that they formerly kept cows, but that it
proved too much trouble. *Crantz's History of Greenland,*
vol. I, p. 74.

[1] *Ramos Hayth* or *Rensoa.*

[2] *Reyne Deer.* This affords another proof that the Icelandic colonies were all situated on the west side of Greenland,
as there are no reindeer on the east coast.

[3] *Stone Fattes.* This material is still found on the west
coast of Greenland, though it is not abundant. In the course
of three hundred years it might well become scarce. The Danish *Rensoa* is distinctly called an island, though the same idea
is conveyed by Hudson's version; the language of which could
only be applied to insulated land.

Item, West from this lyeth another high Land called *The long high Land:*[1] and by another called

——whereon are eight great Orchards,[2] all belong-

Eight
great Or-
chards be-
longing to
the Cathe-
drall
Church.

ing to the Cathedrall Church. But the Tenths thereof they give to the *Warsdell*[3] Church.

Item, next to this Sound lyeth another Sound called *Swaster* Ford,[4] wherein standeth a Church called *Swaster.* This Church belongeth to all this Sound, and to *Romse* Ford,[5] lying next it. In this Sound is a great Garden belonging to the King, called Saint *Henlestate.*[6]

Swaster
Ford.

Item, next to that lyeth *Ericks* Ford,[7] and entring therein lyeth an high Land called *Ericks Hought;*[8]

Ericks
Hought.

---

[1] *Long High Land.* *Langoa,* equivalent to Long Island.

[2] *Orchards* Here again we must remember that we have a Greenlander's idea of a great orchard, which we are taught by the Danish to translate *farms.*

[3] *Warsdell, i. e.,* Wartsdale.

[4] *Swaster Ford,* Hualsefiord from *Hvalsoefjord.*

[5] *Romse Ford.* This should read *Ramstadefiord.*

[6] *Henlestate,* should read *Thiodhildestad.* Rafn thinks it was called thus after the wife of Eric the Red, and says *quæ villa ita probabiliter appellata est a Thjodhilda (populi Bellona vel defensatrice), quod nimirum nomen uxor Eiriki Rufi cum baptismi Christiani sacramento accepit, prius Thorhilda (Thori dei Bellona) vocata.*

[7] *Eries Ford.* Ericsfiord, the home of Eric the Red, the place where he finally found rest from his wandering, and from whose village of Brattalid his sons and daughter sailed in their voyages to New England, sharing the hardship and the honor of the new discoveries with Thorfinn Karlsefne.

[8] *Eries Hought,* or isle.

which pertayneth the one halfe to *Dewers Kerke,*[1] and is the first Parish church on *Groneland,* and lyeth on the left hand as you sayle into *Ericks* Ford : and *Dewers Kerke* belongeth all to *Meydon* Ford, which lyeth North-west from *Ericks* Ford.[2]

—— *Item,* farther out then *Ericks* Ford, standeth a Church called *Skogel Kerke,*[3] which belongeth to all *Skogel Kerke.* *Medford:* And farther in the Sound standeth a Church called *Leaden Kerke.*[4] To this church belongeth all thereabout to the Sea; and also on the other side as farre as *Bowsels.*[5] There lyeth also a great Orchard called *Grote Lead,*[6] in which the *Gusman* (that is a chief or Bayliffe ouer the Boores) doth dwell.

And farther out then *Ericks* Ford, lyeth a Ford or Sound called Fossa, which belongeth to the Cathedrall Church : and the sayd *Fossa* Sound lyeth *Fossa Sound.*

---

[1] *Dewers Kerke.* Dyurenes church. This name, says Rafn, comes from *dyr* a beast, or animal, and means *promontorium animalium.*

[2] *Meydon Ford,* from Mittfjord, signifying Middle-fiord.

[3] *Skogel Kerke,* from *Solefjellds Kierche,* Solefiells Church or Sunny Hills church.

[4] *Leaden Kerke,* from *Leyder Kierche;* the term *Leyder* having a derivation signifying a place of assembly, consultation, or debate.

[5] *Bousels,* from the Danish *Burfielld,* signifying caves of the mountain.

[6] *Grote Lead.* Here we must recognize Brattalid, from *Brattelede,* where the house of Eric the Red stood.

as men sayle out towards *Ericks* Ford : and to the North of it lye two Villages, the one called *Ener Bay*, and the other *Forther Bay*, because they lye so.

Breda Ford.
Larmont Ford.
Ice Dorpe.

Item, from thence farther North lyeth *Breda* Ford,[1] and after that *Larmont* Ford[2] from that West, and from *Larmont* Ford to the West is *Ice* Dorpe.[3] All these are places built, and in them dwell people.

Item, from the Easterbuilded Land to the Wester Dorpe is twelue miles or leagues:[4] and the rest is all waste land. In the Dorpe on the West standeth a Church, which in times past belonged to the Cathedrall Church, and the Bishop did dwell there. But now the *Skerlingers*[5] have all the West

The Sker-lengers.

---

[1] *Breda* Ford, or Bredefiord from *Bredefjord*.

[2] *Lormont Ford*, or Lodmundfiord, from *Lodmundfjord*.

[3] *Ice Dorpe* seems to refer to the region distinguished for its inclemency.

[4] This agrees with the modern examinations of the territories of Greenland. The testimony of the ruins combines with the literary argument to put the East Bygd in the present district of Julian's Hope, or eight days' sail from Iceland. Graah found from the study of both sources of information that the West Bygd began in latitude 62°, 30', almost exactly a six days' boat journey, or one hundred and sixty-eight miles from Immartinek, the most northerly and westerly fiord in Julian's Hope, where ruins are found; or, as Graah says, the West Bygd began close to and north of the ice-blink of Frederic's Hope. See *Graah's Expedition*, p. 165.

[5] *Skerlingers, i. e.*, Skrællings, a term thought by some to mean small men. It is the term always used by the Icelandic writers

Lands and Dorps. And there are now many Horses, Oxen and Kine, but no people, neither Christians nor Heathen : but they were all carried away by the Enemie the *Skerlengers*. Many Horses, Oxen and Kine.

All this before written was done by *Iuer Boty* borne in *Gronland*, a principall man in the Bishops Court : who dwelt there many yeers, and saw and Knew all these places. He was chosen by the whole Land as Captayne, to goe with ships to the Westland, to driue away their enemies the Skerlengers.[1] But hee coming there, found no people, neither Christians nor Heathen, but found there many Sheepe running being wilde, of which Sheep they tooke with them as many as they could carrie, and with them returned to their Houses. This before named *Iuer Boty* was himSelfe with them.[2] *Iuer Boty*, The author.

when speaking of those natives whom they met. See *Pre-Columbian Discovery*, p. 41 *n*.

[1] A tradition of the conflicts between the Icelandic colonists and the natives appears to have been preserved in the account given to Crantz by the natives, who called the men who came to Greenland *Kablunets*, saying that a quarrel arose, which finally terminated in the extinction of the latter. A locality called *Pissiksarbik* is pointed out in the district of Ball's River as the scene of the battle. The name indicates *a place of shooting arrows*. Near by are some old Icelandic ruins. (*Crantz*, vol. I, 204.

[2] Here the original ends, though Prof. Rafn gives four paragraphs by a later hand.

A great Wildernesse called *Hemel Hatsfelt*, to the North of the West land.

To the North[1] of the West Land, lyeth a great Wilderness with Clifes or Rockes, called *Hemel Hatsfelt*.[2] Farther can no man. sayle, because there lye many *Swalgen*[3] or Whirl-pooles; and also for the Water and the Sea.

Mines of Silver, white Beares, white Hawkes, all sorts of fish.

Item, in *Groneland* are many Siluer Hills[4] and many white Beares with red patches[5] on their heads; and also White Hawkes, and all sorts of Fish, as in other Countries.

Item, there is Marble Stone[6] of all colours, also

---

[1] *The North*, the so-called uninhabitable region; though the Northmen penetrated much farther into the polar region, and had a summer station near the mouth of Lancaster Sound. See *Pre-Columbian Discovery*, p. xxxii.

[2] *Hemel Hatsfelt*, from the Danish, *Hemelrachs Fjelld*. Rafn suggests that this is from *Himinraki = cœlum petens vel tangens*. It probably took the name from a pinnacled rock.

[3] *Swalgen*, from *Haffsvallege*.

[4] *Silver Hills*. The things here enumerated are also mentioned in the *Royal Mirror*. These additions to Bardsen's work were not made from a personal knowledge of the country. Graah speaks of the mountainous icebergs as resembling silver hills; but this is probably not what the writer referred to. This touch calls up the style of Spaniards, who wrote after the rediscovery of America by Columbus. Crantz mentions " Cat-Silver."

[5] This statement is from the *Royal Mirror*.

[6] Crantz says, " Of the limestone kind we find on the seaside a good deal of coarse marble of all sorts of colors, but the greatest part black and white, with veins running through it. On the strand we find broken pieces of red marble with white, green, and other veins, which acquire such a polish by the frequent rolling and washing of the waves, that it is not much inferior to the best Italian marble."—*Greenland*, vol. 1, p. 54.

Zeuell stone or the Loadstone,[1] which the fire can not hurt, whereof they make many vessels, as [2] * * * Pots, and other great vessels.[3]

Item, in *Groneland* runneth great streames, and there is much Snow and Ice : But it is not so cold, as it is in *Island* or *Norway*.[4]

Item, there grow on the high Hills, Nuts and Acorns, which are as great as Apples, and good to

Groneland not so cold as Island or Norway.

Fruits.

---

[1] Graah found a rock at Serketnoua, containing a magnetic substance of such intense power as to cause the compass to vary 14°.

[2] There is a blank here in Purchas's version.

[3] We may notice here that Crantz says that this stone is found at Ball's River, where it is quite abundant. It is compounded of clay, and in working falls off like fine flour, making the fingers greasy. It is easily cut, yet ponderous and compact. When rubbed with oil, it becomes very smooth, though exposure to the air renders it porous. The natives cut lamps and kettles from it, while it also makes the best of crucibles. Near Lake Como, the people formerly carried on quite a trade in vessels made of such stone. See *Scheuchzer's Natural History, Switzerland*, P. I., p. 379. Also see *Pring's Natural History*, L. XXIII. c. 22.

[4] Concerning this paragraph it may be said, that the climate of Greenland is extremely variable, and that the cold weather, though severe, does not last but a few days at a time, the severe cold being followed by moderate weather ; while in the summer it is often uncomfortably warm. Sometimes when it is extremely cold in Europe, the winter in Greenland will prove warm. Egede says that in the well known cold winter of 1739–40 there was no ice in the Bay of Disco until March, and that the wild geese went north in January. Crantz thinks that less snow and rain falls in Greenland than in Norway. See *Crantz's Greenland*, vol. I, p. 50.

eat. There groweth also the best Wheate, that can grow in the whole Land.[1]

This Sea Card [2] was found in the Iles of Ferro [3] or farre, lying between *Shot-lant*[4] and *Island*, in an old reckoning Booke, written aboue one hundred yeeres agoe; [5] out of which this was all taken.

Punus and *Potharse.*   *Item, Punnus* and *Potharse,*[6] haue inhabited *Is-*

---

[1] Rafn says, and with reason, that the writer who added these things to the account of Bardsen confounded the productions of Greenland with those of Vinland (New England). Concerning the grains, Crantz says: "The Europeans have several times attempted to sow barley and oats. They grow as fine and as high as in our countries, but seldom advance so far as the ear, and never to maturity."—*Greenland*, vol. i, p. 64.

[2] With the previous paragraph the Danish version of Rafn ends.

[3] Situated north of Scotland, one hundred and seventy miles northwest from Shetland and three hundred and fifty southeast from Iceland. They are twenty-two in number, seventeen being inhabited. The principal is Stromöe. The people are descendants of the Northmen, and speak a dialect of the Norse, though the official language is Danish, as the isles belong to Denmark. The possessor of this "Sea-Card" came by it very naturally.

[4] These, with the Orkneys, were held by Northmen and their descendants.

[5] This, it will be perceived, carries the somewhat modern version from which Hudson's was translated, back to the period of Columbus. All that follows appears to be of the same age as the Faroe version of Bardsen. At what time it reached Holland we are unable to conjecture, though a copy of the treatise was probably in the hands of John Skolnus, and by him may have been communicated to the Spanish or Portuguese by whom he was known.

[6] The writer here, it must be remembered, is not Bardsen, but one who knew much less about Iceland. We are at a loss for an

land ceertayne yeers, and sometimes haue gone to Sea, and haue had their trade in *Groneland*. Also *Punnus* did give the *Islanders* their Lawes, and caused them to bee written, Which Laws doe continue to this day in *Island*, and are called by name *Punnus* Lawes.

The Course from Island to Groneland.

IF men bee South from the Hauen of *Bred* Ford in *Island*, they shall sayle West, till they see *Whitsarke* vpon *Grone land*, and then sayl somewhat South west, till *Whitsarke* bee North off you, and so you need nor fear Ice, but may boldly sayle to *Whitsarke*, and from thence to *Ericks* Hauen.

If men bee North the Hauen of Bredford in *Island*, then sayle South west, till *Whitsarke* beare North : then sayl to it, and so come to *Ericks* Hauen.

---

account of *Punnus* and *Potharse*. The laws of Iceland were drawn up by Ulflijot and Grim Geitskor in the year 928, after the former had spent three years with Thorleif the wise in Norway. In Arngrim Jonas' account of Iceland (Part II, sec. 1.) we find the following : " In the year 1050 it was decreed in a solemn assembly of the inhabitants, that temporal or political laws (the constitutions whereof being brought out of Norway were communicated to the Icelanders by Uflijot in the year 926 [?]) should everywhere give place to the canon of Divine law."

Trolebo-thon.

If you see Ice, that cometh out of *Trolebothon*,[1] you shall go more Southerly, but not too far South for feare of Freesland,[2] for there runneth an hard Streame, And it is fifteen miles or leagues from Fresland.

Item, Freesland lyeth South, and *Island* East from *Gronland*.

Item, from the Ice that hangeth on the Hilles in *Gronland*, commeth a great Foggs, Frost and Cold.

Trolebo-thon, a great Wilderness.

And such a Fogge cometh out of the Ice of *Trolebothon:* and it is a great Wilderness.

The commodities of Gronland.

There are Sables, Marternes, Hermelens, or Ermins, White Beares, and White Hawkes, Seales,

---

[1] *Trolebothen.* In the former part of the treatise, this is called the *Long North Bottome.* The Danish there is *Botnen*, for which Rafn gives *Trollebotnen.*

[2] The whole subject of Frisland has often been treated as a mystery. Asher, however, gives a solution. The Venetian brothers are reported to have visited Frisland, Engroneland, Iceland and Estotiland in 1387. Their chart, the original of which still exists, was derived from the Scandinavians. Nearly the whole of the northwestern part of Jodocus Hondius's map was copied from it. Still this map of the Zeni brothers was very imperfect, Iceland not being so well drawn as Greenland. Frisland also is badly depicted, being located where no land was ever known, so that the only explanation to be given is that they confounded Frisland with the Faroe Islands. This led to the appearance of Frisland, in subsequent maps as a separate country lying in the sea south-west of Iceland. No one questioned its existence, and down to a late period it was usually represented. Frobisher had a copy of the Zeni chart, but owing to lines of latitude and longitude placed upon it by later hands was led in several mistakes.

White and gray, Gold and Siluer Hills, also Fish dryed and salted, and thousands of Salmons: also store of Losh Hides and other Hides. There are Hares, Foxes, Wolues, Otters and Veltfrasen.

Now if it please God they come to *Gronland*, then shall they let but two men on shoare; who will take with them diuers kinds of Marchandize: and let them deale with good order, and let them be such as can make good Reports, what they there doe see or finde; and let them observe whether men may Land there or no, with the loue of the Inhabitants. And I counsaile and

---

The southern point of Greenland is in latitude 60°, but the added lines made it appear in 65°; accordingly, when, in July, 1577, he came upon the Greenland coast in latitude 61°, he supposed that he had reached Frisland. He therefore reports that the map of Zeni suited the country well, whereas the land seen was the southern part of Greenland. Davis also came in sight of the coast in latitude 61°, but finding that this was the wrong latitude for Frisland, concluded that this was a new discovery, and called it Desolations. Touching the coast again in latitude 64°, he concluded that Desolations was an island, not having seen the line of coast between. Thus Desolations came to have a distinct existence on the map, and when Hudson says that he "raised Desolations," he means the land south of what he has marked as Greenland on his map. *Busse Land* laid down on many old charts east of Desolations had a still less real existence; one of Frobisher's ships, the *Busse*, meeting large fields of ice there, which were mistaken for an island. See *Asher*, p. clxv. Of course, the subsequent searches made for an island of ice, were unsuccessful. The popular idea which afterwards prevailed was that the land was sunk by an earthquake.

charge those that shall trade for Gronland, that they set no more folks on Land, but they keep men enough to man the Ship. And looke well to the course you do hold to *Gronland*, that if those that bee set on shoare be taken, they may come home again with God's helpe. For if shipping returne, they may come home or bee released in a yeere and a day. And in your living there so demean yourselues to them, that in time you may win the Countrey and the people.[1]

Good counsell for trauelling to *Gronland*. Remember my Scholar and Clearke, which shall there bee appointed as Commander, that you send those on Land, that will show themselues diligent Writers, and that they carrie themselues so, that they may learn thereby the State of the Countrey. They shall take with them two Boats and Eight Tynder-boxes for fire. Oares, and take Tynder-boxes for fire if there be no Habitation. Also set vp Crosses of Wood or Stone, if need be.

---

[1] In reading the foregoing we are forcibly reminded of the general neglect of the true policy by Hudson, in common with most navigators and settlers, which neglect has cost so much blood and treasure. In the account of Hudson's third voyage we have the following: " In the morning we manned our scute with four muskets and sixe men, and tooke one of their shallops and brought it aboard. We then manned our scute with twelve men and muskets, and two stone pieces or murderers, and drave the savages from their houses, and took the spoyle of them, as they would have done of us." *Asher's Henry Hudson*, p. 61.

This Note following was found in an old Booke of
Accounts, in the Yeere 1596.

IN *primis*, From *Gtad*, in Norway, standing
neere the Latitude of sixtie three Degrees,[1] Courses for Gronland.
you shall hold your course due West: and that
course will bring you upon *Swartnesse*, in *Gronland*.
And in this course is the least streame and least
perill of *Swalgen* or *Indrafts*. There is lesse perill
this way, then is on the North-side; you shall
keep ⅔ of the sea on Freeseland side, and one
third on *Island* side. And if it bee cleere weather,
and you haue kept your course right West, you
shall see the Mount of *Sneuel Iokul*[2] in the South-
west part of *Island*. And if you have a storme in A Storme in the North.
the North, you must shunne it as you can, till
Whitsarke bee North of you. Then shall you Whitsarke.
sayle right with it, and seeke the Land: and you
shall find a good Hauen, called *Ericks* Ford. Ericks Ford.

Item, If you bee between *Gronland* and *Island*,
you may see *Sneuels Iokul* on *Island* and *Whitsarke*

---

[1] Here we have the first indication of modern science to be
found in these sailing directions; though immediately after
Freesland is mentioned.

[2] *Sneuel Iokul*, or Snæfellsjökul. A *jökul* is a mountain per-
petually covered with snow.

on *Gronland*, if it be cleere weather. Therefore men of experience doe assume that it is but thirtie leagues betweene both.

Also if you haue a storm between *Gronland* and *Island*, you must haue care you bee not laid on *Freesland*[1] with the Streame and Winde; for the Streame or Current doth run strong vpon *Frees-land* out of the North.

Also if you haue a storme out of the South, you shall not sayle out of your course, but keepe it as neere as you can possibly, till *Whitsarke* in *Gron-land* beare North of you: then sayle towards it, and you shall come into *Ericks* Ford, as it is afore-said in the first Article.

---

[1] *Freesland.* We must note here again that this is by a modern writer. Frisland does not appear in anything that Ivar Bardsen, or any other Icelander or Greenlander wrote.

Ivar Bardsen's Sea Card, translated from Prof.
Rafn's version.

[*Antiquitates Americanæ*, p. 300.]

Men of understanding born in Greenland say
that from the north of Stad in Norway to the
east coast of Iceland called Horn is seven days
sail west.

Item. From Snæfellsness on the west coast of
Iceland the distance to Greenland is shortest, and
it is said to be two days and two nights sail westward. Then Gunnbiorn's Rocks lie half way between Iceland and Greenland. This course was
anciently taken, but now it is said there is ice on
the rocks that has come out of the Northern Ocean,
so that it is no longer possible to go that way
without peril of life, as will afterwards be seen.

Item. From Langeness which is on the north-
east of Iceland to the above said Horn-ness, it is
two days and two night's sail to Sualbarde in
Haffsbotnen.

Item. They who sail the course from Bergen to
Greenland, without coming to Iceland, hold west
until they come in the region of Reikianess south
of the promontory of Iceland, from which they
should then be distant twelve Icelandic sea miles

south, and then, keeping the same westerly course, steer for that part of Greenland which is called Huarf. The day before the said Huarf is seen, will be seen another snow mountain called Huidserk; and between these two mountains and Huarf and Huidserk lies a ness called Heriulfsness and near it is a harbor called Sandhaven, where merchants were wont to come.

Item. In sailing from Iceland you must take your departure from Snæfellsness, which lies at a distance of twelve sea-miles north-west from Reikianess, and shape a course to the west for a day and a night, and then to the south-west until you have passed all the ice above mentioned lying at and around Gunnbiorn's Rocks. You must then steer north-west for a day and a night which will bring you to Huarf in Greenland, where Heriulfsness and Sandhaven are situated.

Item. The most eastern district in Greenland is situated straight east from Heriulfsness, and is called Skagafiord, and it is a village.

Item. East of Skagafiord is a bay called Bearsfiord which is not dwelt in. At the mouth of the bay is a long risse lying across the inlet so that large ships cannot harbor in it. There are many whales and much hunting for them, though not without the bishop's consent, as the fishery belongs to the Cathedral Church. And in this bay is a large whirlpool, in which whirlpool the whales run in when the tide runs out.

Item. East of Bearsfiord is another haven called the Longest-of-All, which at the mouth is narrow, but farther in very wide. The length of it is so great that the end of it is not known. There is no current. It contains many little islands. There are many birds and eggs, and it is plain land on both sides covered with grass.

Item. A little further towards the east from the ice mountain there is a port called Finsbudr, from the name of a page of Saint Olaf who with many others was wrecked here. And those that were saved buried those that were drowned, and on their graves they set great stone crosses, where they stand to this day.

Still farther east towards the ice mountains, is a great island called Cross, where there are many white bears, which cannot be hunted without permission of the Bishop, as the island belongs to the Cathedral. Beyond it to the east nothing is to be seen at sea or on the shore but ice and snow.

Item. Now we shall return to the affairs already touched upon concerning the Greenland colony.

Item. On the East side of Heriulfsness is a colony called Ketilsfiord, which is well built. Sailing into the fiord you see on the right hand its mouth, into which a great flood runs. Opposite the mouth stands a church called Auroos Church, consecrated to the Cross, which church holds all the islands, rocks, and things thrown up by the sea, without as far as Heriulfsness, and those within as far as the Bay of Peter.

Item. At the Bay of Peter is a large habitable tract called Wartsdale, before which tract is a large lake, twelve sea miles long, abounding in fish. The Church of Peter holds the tract of Wartsdale.

Item. Near this place is a great monastery dwelt in by regular canons, which is consecrated to Saint Olaf and Saint Augustine. The monastery holds all interior lands to the end of the bay, and all those on the outside.

Item. Next to Ketilsfiord is Rafnsfiord, in the interior of which lies a cloister of nuns of Saint Benedict's Order. This cloister holds all the interior lands to the end of the bay and the exterior part as far as the Voge Church, dedicated to Saint Olaf the king. In this bay are many little islands, one-half of which belong to Voge Church, and the other half is held by the Cathedral Church. In these little islands are many hot springs, which in winter are so hot that no one can approach them, but in summer they are more temperate, so that many bathing in them are cured of disease. And near this is Einarsfiord, between which and the aforementioned Rafnsfiord is a great garden called the Foss, which belongs to the king. Here stands a splendid church dedicated to Saint Nicholas, to which the king appoints priests. Next to this is a great lake, abounding in fish, which, after rising with tides and rains, flows back leaving a great number of fish on the sand. And when you sail out of Einarsfiord to the left is a branch of the sea called Thorvaldsvike. And somewhat above in the same fiord is a promontory called Klining. Beyond this is another branch called Granevig; above which is a large garden called Daler, which is held by the Cathedral Church. On the right when sailing out of the fiord is a great forest, which is the property of the Cathedral, in which forest all the great and small cattle are pastured. The Cathedral Church holds all Einarsfiord and a great island called Rensoa, that lies before Einarsfiord, where in the autumn season many rein-deer resort, and which they commonly hunted, though not without the permission of the bishop. In this same island are the softest stones to be found in all Greenland, of which they make pots and vessels, which on account of their durability the fire will not injure. And from one rock they made vessels that hold ten or twelve tuns.

And far west from this lies another long island, called Langey, on which are eight great farms.

The Cathedral Church holds the whole island
except a tenth, which belongs to the Wartsdale
church. And next to Einarsfiord is Hualsefiord,
in which is a church called Hualsefiord's, which
with the fiord and all adjacent belongs to Kamb-
stadfiord. In this fiord is a royal garden called
Thiodhildestad.

And next to this is Ericsfiord in the mouth of
which is an island called Erics Island, part of
which belongs to the Cathedral Church and part
to the Church of Dyurenes. The Church of Dyurenes is the principal church in Greenland, and
stands on the left hand entering Ericsfiord. All
of Medfiord are under Dyurenes Church; Medfiord extends north-west from Ericsfiord. Far
from thence in Ericsfiord is Solefields Church,
which belongs to Midfiord. Far in the interior of
the fiord is a church called Leyder Church. To
this church belongs all to the end of the bay and on
the other side as far as Burfielld. All from the
outside of Burfielld is owned by the Cathedral
Church. There is also situated a great orchard
called Brattelid, where the Bailif lives.

Farther out from Langoa are four islands, called
Lamboer, or Lambornse, thus called, because they
lie between Langoa and Lamboer. Before the
middle part of Ericsfiord is another narrow fiord
called Fossafiord. The islands enumerated belong

to the Cathedral Church before mentioned situated in Fossafiord in the middle of Ericsfiord.

And north opposite Ericsfiord are two branches of the sea of which one is called the Exterior and the other the Interior, by which names they are known.

And near by northward is Breidafiord, in which fiord is Medfiord. Hence far northward is Eyafiord; next to this is Borgafiord, after which is Lodmundfiord, then Isefiord, which is the most western of the fiords in the East district. The islands are all occupied by settlers.

And between the East and the West Bygd it is twelve sea miles, the whole extent of which is waste lands. In the west Bygd stands a splendid church, called Stennes Church where in former times was the bishop's seat. Now the Skrællings hold all the country west; it is nevertheless full of horses, goats, oxen, sheep, and all the animals are wild. There are no inhabitants, neither Christians nor Pagans.

Item. Ivar Bardson, a Greenlander, of Garda, the Episcopal seat of Greenland, who was Bailiff many years, related these to us, having himself seen all these things before related, and been one among them. He was selected as captain to go to the West Bygd to drive thence the Skrællings. And when they came there there were no men neither Christians nor Pagans, but a great many wild sheep and cattle, of which they put some on board their vessels and brought them to their homes. One of the men was Ivar above mentioned.

Item. Far to the north of the West Bygd is a great mountain called Hemelrachi, beyond which it is not advisable to sail, on account of many whirlpools by which all the sea is filled.

Item. Greenland has many silver mountains and many white bears with red spots on their heads, white falcons, whales teeth and many fish such as abound in all lands. There is also marble stone of all colors, soft rocks, that are not injured by fire, from which the Greenlanders make pots, urns, vases and vats of ten or twelve tuns capacity. There is also an abundance of rein-deer.

Item. In Greenland there are never great tempests.

Item. In Greenland there is much snow; there it is not so cold as in Iceland and Norway. On the tops of the hills there grow alders, and fruits of the size of large apples and very sweet. There is also found the best of wheat.

NOTE.— Line 14, page 18, for " When," *read* " Before."
The statement in the same paragraph depends upon the calculation of Hudson, who put the latitude of the place in 44° 1'.

INDEX.

13